Not in the Box

Elizabeth Wells

DEDICATION

I want to dedicate this book to my husband, Ian, my children, parents, uncles, aunts, cousins, and all those who stood with me when I faced death.
All I can say is thank you.

ACKNOWLEDGMENTS

I wanted to acknowledge all the NHS staff who at every stage of my journey went above and beyond to help me and my family. And, to the work of the NHS blood and transplant service who help people every day to do something extraordinary in donating their blood and organs. If it wasn't for the selfless act of a family consumed with their own grief, donating their loved one's organs.
I simply wouldn't be here today.

'In being presented with the fragility of life and looking through the lens of my own mortality, I discovered it wasn't death that I feared. What filled me with dread was the idea of my life ending without having achieved my full potential. I was confronted with the overwhelming realisation that everyday really did matter.'

Elizabeth Wells 2023

CHAPTER 1

Life has its ups and downs; it is full of celebrations and goodbyes. We all experience happy times, and difficult times. Sometimes the chaos and noise can be so overwhelming that we feel like we just want to curl up in bed and hide from the world. But what happens when drawing the curtains, escaping in a film, or reassuring words don't even begin to address the all-consuming fear of failure, of pain, or death? What do you do when any form of relief, let alone comfort, seems so distant?

When you suddenly receive news that is so powerfully destructive, it completely derails you from the path you were following, throwing you into a raging tornado from which there is no escape. Standing powerless, helpless to your own destruction and demise as it seeks to destroy everything you hold dear, lacking any ability to stop its mighty force. You watch as an observer as it tears up everything of any value and exposes the very foundations on which your life's structures were built.

There were areas of hurt and trauma in my life that, rather than choosing to address, I instead build a bridge over enabling me to continue my journey seemingly unaffected. So long as the flow of traffic was restored and I successfully portrayed a fully functioning and well-balanced life, I could continue to live, regardless of the warning signs.

As I had journeyed through life, weathering the storms, I had failed to see that the construction of seemingly inconsequential defense mechanisms had only resulted in my life becoming a series of bridges in a rapidly expanding jungle. The more problems and issues I faced, the more bridges I built to cover them.

The bridges grew higher and more perilous until one day a weather system like no other moved in. The storm clouds gathered, and the skies became dark and menacing, the wind shaking every structure to its core. The only option left was to hide from the impending doom and devastation, only daring to open my eyes when the eye of the storm, at its peak, offered momentary respite.

Caught in the eye of the storm, a brief pause in my never-ending state of misery. A chance to assess the damage. Evaluating the magnitude of the destruction only to find that I was once again sat amongst the rubble of that first bridge. It was then I realised that no matter how clever I was with its design or how strong I built the structure, the problems and the storms of life would always come to weaken it. So, when the day came that a hurricane, a tornado, and a tsunami hit all at once, it tore everything down, until I was left with the only thing that ever really mattered, my life.

Growing up I thought that my family dynamics were, well, normal. As is the case with all children, the environment in which you're placed to grow is the only one you know. It's not until later in life that you realise that maybe things weren't entirely okay. Whilst parts of my childhood would have been viewed as good, it wasn't until I entered a loving relationship of my own that I realised that living in an atmosphere of pal papule tension wasn't normal and it certainly wasn't an arena that I wanted to replicate for my children to grow up in.

Facing a life storm of my own, I now not only wanted to but needed to explore family dynamics. Through the lens of my own personal experiences and also from a more informed and professional perspective. Putting all the emotion to one side, if only for a moment, so I could explore the facts and identify the truth in an attempt to understand the cause of many of the storms that had entered my life.

I wanted to explore if the damage they inflicted could have been minimised or stopped through my actions and inactions, or if I was always destined to ride the roller coaster of life that I had been placed on. Although I always had an underlying knowing that things weren't ok growing up, I feared that the process of uncovering this might expose a truth that would not only destroy me but those around me. I did what many of us do and put it in a box marked do not open... EVER!

It wasn't until I was in my early forties and recovering from a life-saving liver transplant that I realised it was time to reach up lift that particular, box off the shelf and unpack it. My parents had split when I was in my late teens and the fall out and hurt from the experience had haunted me ever since. My life had been thrown into chaos and I had spent the following twenty plus years battling a depression and inner anguish that had, on so many occasions, very nearly destroyed me.

Now on the other side of a journey that had resulted in me nearly losing my life, I knew that I had no other option but to sort through this in my mind. I had been given a second chance at life. The gift of a donor had enabled me to live and I wasn't about to live life 2.0 with all the debilitating baggage that had so nearly put me in a box six feet under.

This isn't the first time that I have tried to unpack it. I had some years ago completed additional study as a specialist family nurse, which involved delving into the psychology of relationships and family. It was then that I realised, what I had experienced growing up was not okay and it had positioned me on a path of self-destruction. People who are hurting don't make good decisions, especially when all their support networks are pulled from them.

When I first got taken ill it was a complete shock. I understood I was no saint, but I was also no worse than the majority of working parents in the western world. I worked hard, did my best to raise my children, and I was relatively successful. I was happily married, and my five children were all thriving. I had been through some really, stressful times, but I had walked out the other side, maybe with a few more scars and battle wounds than I would have liked, but I survived! And that's all that mattered, right?

I was still walking and had managed to pick myself up whilst supporting the others around me through the disasters that seemed to periodically hit my family's life. But rather than mending the damage inflicted by the storm, I had buried it, built a bridge over it. The truth was I hadn't taken the best care of myself. I had, in thinking I was doing the right thing, put the needs of my family first which on the surface isn't a bad thing but it had resulted in me neglecting myself and burying my own needs.

I was now painfully addressing the question of whether my need to put others first stemmed from hurt that I had experienced. My mum had left me in my teens with my dad to, as I saw it, pursue a new life that didn't involve me or in any way meet my needs. She sought to simply fulfil her own desires without any thought of how that might impact what should have been so precious to her, her own children.

Hindsight is a wonderful thing, and as I sat recovering, I was given the chance to reflect. The surgeon only weeks before had told my husband, as I lay in coma post-surgery, that I had come within two hours of dying. There had been complications with the initial transplant surgery which had involved me bleeding heavily and being rushed back into theatre for a further five-hour emergency surgery to prevent me bleeding out and losing my life. Eight liters of blood, five days in a coma, two weeks in intensive care and a month in hospital would not only save my life but change the way I saw the world. Donating your loved one's body for the benefit of others when you are consumed with your own grief, pushing aside your own needs and wants to contemplate the needs of people that you don't even know and never will - now that's love. And it gave me the motivation and drive I needed to live life differently.

I was beginning to realise that decisions I had made in my life were rooted in past hurt and a determination that my children would never be made to feel the way I had. Unloved, worthless, rejected and abandoned. However, this had led me to make some terrible choices and I had failed to realise at times the need to put boundaries in place to protect myself and those around me.

Staying healthy in the future was not just about taking care of my physical health, but just as my toxic, diseased liver had been removed and replaced with a healthy one, I now needed to do the same with my mental and spiritual self. I had no choice but to go though the most painful experience of my life in undergoing two surgeries after months of agonising physical and mental anguish, it as painful as it was giving me a lifeline another chance at life. With my physical health now on the road to recovery, I knew that I needed to perform a surgery of sorts on my mental health, and drill down to remove the toxic hurt that had happened so long ago it had become embedded in the foundations of my entire life.

I had been through a war of sorts, and I had been severely wounded, a shrapnel wound on the surface can look minor but the pain and trauma it can cause can be agonising and it needs to be removed. By exploring what had gone wrong and addressing why, or at the very least reaching a level of understanding, I could begin to rid myself of the paralysis caused by this trauma, hurt and rejection.

The good news was it wasn't as powerful as it had been. Life events had enabled me to unearth parts of it in the past. Some of the bridges had already been blown up or dismantled. So, it certainly didn't have the hold on me that it once did. But there were still fragments, still behaviours that those around me had chosen to burden me with at my most vulnerable moments. I realised I now had an opportunity to rebuild a foundation that wasn't based on trauma but on the truth that I was loved and valuable. Precious enough to be given a second chance of life and was something I would treasure forever.

Chapter Two

Nine months ago, I was feeling tired and not as healthy as I wanted to be. However, I was still active and had enjoyed camping with my family that summer. Never in a million years would I have believed that within a few months I would be fighting for my life. Nevertheless, I was about to be a dealt a blow that would certainly derail me and change the direction of my life forever.

Shortly after returning from our summer holiday camping, I had woken a few times in the night not feeling very well. I felt exhausted and just couldn't shake the feeling of tiredness and lethargy which I had been feeling for weeks; the summer holiday hadn't quenched the exhaustion at all. Worse still, I had pain in my abdomen that wasn't present before the holiday. However hard I tried I just couldn't get comfortable. I was woken from my sleep around 2AM with what I thought was indigestion, so I made my way downstairs to the kitchen and poured myself a glass of cold milk. I'd always liked milk and found that it often helped if I was suffering with excess acid or a bit of heartburn. Perhaps, unknowingly, I also found some comfort from a simple glass of milk.

The milk didn't work. If anything, it just made me feel a little sick. I took some paracetamol and made my way back upstairs to bed. It was the early hours and I needed to try to get some sleep, or I would be tired in the morning. My husband, Ian and I had run a business from our home for some years now. It allowed us to fit our lives around the needs of the children and, having survived the pandemic, we had recently opened our own retail shop. We couldn't afford to have sick days. If orders had come in online overnight, then they needed to be fulfilled.

The morning came and the pain intensified. My whole body ached as if I had some sort of flu without the cold symptoms. I was never one for going to the doctors, especially since the pandemic. According to the news it was a near impossibility to even get an appointment. Yet somehow, I knew that I couldn't ignore this, I ached and hurt in a way I never had. Reluctantly, I called the surgery and to my surprise they wanted to see me almost straight away.

My daughter Katelyn was at home that day, because of the pandemic she had decided to stay at home for university which meant that she was often at home to help out. Seeing how unwell I was she suggested that she drove me to the appointment to save me driving myself.

As we pulled up outside the doctors, despite it now being sometime since the pandemic, they were still exercising extreme caution and only allowing the patient in the building. I suggested that Katelyn stay in the car whilst I popped in, I told her I shouldn't be too long as it looked like they didn't want people in the doctor's surgery longer than was necessary.

As I walked in, I was greeted with hand sanitizer, handed a mask, and asked to take a seat. I walked into the waiting room and saw that the seats were arranged in lines with large spaces in between, to adhere to social distancing in an attempt, to limit the spread of any disease or illness.

As I sat waiting to see the doctor, I rationalised in my head that the symptoms I had were more than likely due to the intense and prolonged stress that we had been under. If navigating the covid crisis with five children and a business that had to cease trading during the lockdowns hadn't been bad enough, the economic decline post-pandemic had nearly seen our business go under. Ian and I had worked seven days a week for longer than I can remember, adapting our business in an attempt to stay afloat.

Ian and I had been through more than our fair share of disasters in our lives, to the extent that we thought we were resilient and hardened to the trials and adversities of life. A decade before, during the global financial crisis, we had lost a business and our home and literally found ourselves on the street with our children. We did what we always did, worked hard, pulled our family close and rode out the storm. We knew that, if nothing else, we would get through the other side with the opportunity to build character and learn valuable life lessons.

Even though we were able to rebuild and protect our children from a lot of the pain that the bankruptcy caused, after several years of trauma, we were now bearing the scars both physical and psychological which were also combined with vivid memories and nightmares that neither of us wanted to revisit.

When unexpectedly faced with an all too familiar situation of uncertainty and potential looming disaster after the Covid virus hit, we all sat in silence as we watched the breaking news on the T.V from our front room. The Prime Minister ordered everyone to stay at home and businesses to shut. My mind raced to process what was going on. Could this all be happening again?

We were again hit by a set of circumstances that were beyond our control, suddenly we were severed from our only income stream. Fear gripped us, we could foresee our whole pack of cards collapsing and once again having to pick up the fragments of what was left and trying our best to continue. I don't think either of us could face the prospect of that happening again, so we relentlessly and tirelessly worked, harder than ever before.

We successfully battled through and saved the business by moving all our direct sales online, but it had taken its toll and we were both very tired and desperately in need of a break.

My mind was brought back into focus as my name was called and I was guided in to see the doctor. He ran through my medical history which was fairly brief. As far as I was concerned, apart from being a little out of shape and battered from the years of tireless work, generally I was fit and well. I explained that we had our struggles like any other family but on the whole life was good.

After discussing my current symptoms, which compromised of an intensifying radiating pain across my abdomen, a slight temperature, and some generalised swelling of my stomach - which I put down to bloating from having a summer full of BBQ's and treats - the doctor took my blood pressure and other vital signs.

He asked me to lay down on the examination bed in the corner of the room, I lifted my top to expose my stomach for him to examine as he began to place his hands and apply varying amounts of pressure on my stomach. It seemed as if he wanted to check and tap every part of my stomach, once he had checked one spot, he moved his hands to another and so on until he had checked it all. It all seemed to be going well until the doctor put pressure on the top of my stomach and the resulting pain exploded throughout my body. I felt as if I was going to hit the ceiling.

Despite remaining very calm the doctor explained that I needed to go to the hospital. I responded by telling him that my daughter was waiting outside and could take me straight over. He interrupted my plan by explaining that I was too poorly to take the 30-minute drive without a medical professional, and he was going to call an ambulance.

With this news he gave me a large brick like device which had a red button on it, I was to sit on the bed and press the button if I felt worse. He left me momentarily to call the paramedics. I took the opportunity to call Katelyn and ask her to come into the examination room. I explained that she would need to come through the waiting room to where I was.

Katelyn appeared some minutes later and I repeated what the doctor had said. As the words exited my mouth it was as if I was in a blur, like my mind was present but encased in a type of fluid. Everything slowed down and felt numb, as if I was being suspended between reality and some kind of alternative state. Maybe it was my mind's way of dealing with uncertainty or illness or infection spreading through by body. Whatever it was, it didn't feel right, and I certainly wasn't okay. I felt poorly, absent and now very scared.

The doctor returned and explained that I need intravenous antibiotics as soon as possible and only the hospital could administer them. In the meantime, he gave me some antibiotics in tablet form. He explained that whilst the paramedics had assured him that an ambulance would be with us as soon as possible, the National Health Service in the U.K was currently at breaking point and the ambulance service was being stretched well beyond reasonable capacity. His plan was to give them a little longer to arrive but any longer and he would arrange to take me by car himself. The seriousness and gravity of the situation was beginning to hit me like a sledgehammer of emotion. Katelyn tried to be as positive as she could but she too looked worried.

Much to the doctor's relief the ambulance arrived. The paramedics were positive and made me feel safe as they strapped me to the trolley bed, and we began the journey to the hospital. They monitored my vital signs continuously as we drove through what was now rush hour traffic. I looked at the monitor, my heart rate and blood pressure were ridiculously high. Although I hadn't practised for a few years, I was a qualified nurse and began to worry. This *really* wasn't good. There was no reason for them to be reading that high. Sure, I was anxious, but this was ridiculous.

As we approached the hospital, I encountered the same scenes that had been on the news over the past few weeks; the ambulances were backed up and queued as they patiently waited in turn to get their patient into the Accident and Emergency department to be seen by a doctor.

So much had happened so quickly, I hadn't had a chance to call Ian, who was working in our retail shop and oblivious to the situation that was unfolding. I called him from the back of the ambulance and, after getting over the initial shock, he raced to be with me at the hospital.

After hours of waiting, I was wheeled on my bed into a bay in the hospital to have bloods and initial assessments taken. Unfortunately, there still wasn't any room for me in the hospital so I was returned to the ambulance under the care of the paramedics who administered fluids, antibiotics and, to my relief, pain meds.

I drifted in and out of sleep, after some time Ian arrived and was allowed to sit with me in the back of the ambulance. He was clearly worried and frustrated that I had not yet been properly admitted to the hospital. He chatted to the paramedics, and they explained the dire situation at the accident and emergency department had been going on for at least two years and there seemed to be no hope of anything getting better. The government refused to acknowledge the issue, let alone help. It had been so bad recently that the previous weekend the whole county, which spanned 80 miles, had only one free ambulance to answer all emergency call outs. In short, if you had a heart attack or stroke you were as good as dead. There was no help.

After sixteen hours in the back of the ambulance and now on my third shift of paramedics, they finally had a bed for me in accident and emergency. After being assessed by the doctors I was told that I would have to stay in. They told me I had developed an infection in my gallbladder and that was causing the pain and abnormal blood results and I would be admitted to a ward to be treated with antibiotics, pain relief and fluids.

Chapter Three

After some time on a trolley in accident and emergency, a bed became available on a ward. I was relieved to be moved away from the chaos of the accident and emergency department. The staff were doing the best they could, but they were clearly overwhelmed by the sheer number of people that needed treatment. There were people everywhere and I feared that I was going to be lost in a sea of patients, some of which quite clearly needed to be treated far more urgently than me.

As I arrived to my allocated bed, I looked around at the other patients on the ward. They were far older than I was by at least twenty years. They all looked so poorly, all I wanted to do was ask for the exit. There was a good reason why I stuck clear of these places, they were so clinical, and you could just smell the lack of hope and the stench of impending death. I put my headphones on that Ian had bought in for me and tried my best to drown everything out with positive music. I was feeling poorly enough as it was, and my now dismal surroundings were not helping my mood at all. Thankfully it wasn't too long before I was seen by the doctors who informed me that I was to go for several scans so they could confirm their diagnosis of a gallbladder infection and double check if there was anything else of significance going on.

I was pleased they were going to check me out. Now that they had sorted me out with some comprehensive pain relief I was, for the first time in days, feeling a lot more comfortable which I was extremely thankful for. The results of the scans came back, and the doctors informed me they had confirmed the presence of gallstones but reassured me that the infection had now been treated and the stones themselves could be treated with medication, I just had to make sure that I ate a low-fat healthy diet. I was so relieved; the ward was full to capacity, and it was obvious that they wanted to discharge anyone they could before the weekend.

Before too long, despite still being in a little pain, they said that I could go home. Ian picked me up, he was so relieved that it was nothing too serious and I was so thankful to be back in more comfortable surroundings.

As I sat in the front room watching tv, I was desperately trying to get comfortable on the sofa. I tried to take my mind off the nausea that was beginning to consume me; I reasoned that it was probably due to lack of sleep and all the antibiotics I had in hospital. I tried my best to ignore it but my whole body ached and I still, despite being home, felt so desperately ill.

Out of nowhere I was struck with the most painful cramp in my legs, it was almost unbearable. I scrambled to get up off the sofa as quickly as possible as the pain radiated through my legs. I tried pacing up and down to try and relax my muscles which were now spasming and sending shooting pain throughout my body. The pain became so intense that I could hardly bear putting my feet on the ground to stand. Ian and the kids were concerned.

"What is it?" Ian asked looking worried.

"I don't know, maybe its cramp" I replied.

"I'm hoping that it will just go if I walk it off. I've not been very active for a few days, maybe that's what caused it", I was trying to reassure them.

The truth was I had never experienced anything like the pain I was in before. I took myself into the hallway to try and walk the pain off and to be away from the looks of worried distress which radiated from the faces of those I loved the most.

My legs began to swell, I ignored it at first in some misplaced hope that this was all one big nightmare that in a moment I would wake up and realise I had just been dreaming. However, as much as I wished otherwise, this was not a dream. It was a very painful reality. Within a couple of hours my legs ballooned, filling with fluid. They became hard, red and my ancles and feet had begun to swell and hurt. My heart began to race I was in such pain, and the worry of what on earth was wrong with me began to intensify as my nose began to bleed.

Tears began to run down my face as the fear of the unknown consumed me. Ian became increasingly alarmed and insisted that we go back to the hospital. That was the last place I wanted to go. But with the pain getting worse there was no other option. The pain became unbearable, sitting and bending became excruciatingly painful. Ian did his best to help me into the car, we both knew it was pointless calling for an ambulance. And after all, what if was just cramp? I questioned myself, maybe I was just tired, and this was all just one big overreaction. With the health service on its knees wasn't I just going to be adding to it? And what would I say? Oh, by the way you only discharged me earlier today after treating me, but now I have cramp! Wouldn't I look like a fool? The questions in my mind continued and I could feel my anxiety building and my heart pounding faster and faster.

My body felt every bump in the road as Ian raced me to the emergency department. By the time we got there my legs had swollen so much that it was agony attempting to get out of the car. I staggered into the entrance of the hospital and was confronted with a barrage of people who were either high or completely intoxicated with alcohol.

It was a Friday night; the whole place was carnage. Thankfully as I had only been discharged some hours before I was triaged quickly, and my name was soon called to see a rather harassed, obviously overworked doctor. My anxiety was sky high and as a result my nose was again gushing with blood, only adding to an already stressful situation.

The doctor's bedside manner was not at all

comforting. He looked at my notes and blood results stating that I should never have been discharged with results like mine. I wasn't sure if I should apologise for the hospital's failings, I was in agony and his attitude was not helping. I asked him what was wrong with me. I was so worried. I had never felt like this, ever. His response was short and to the point.

"Liver Failure".

The words were dipped in a poison that was designed to rip my very soul in two. With those two cold words he had, in an instant, delivered me a death sentence. A numbness descended and a lump formed in my throat but there were no tears, just an inability to communicate anything that would make any sense. All the pain drained as a kind of paralysis griped every fibre of my being.

Ian and I were told to go back in the waiting room while they arranged a bed for me. We both sat quietly for what seemed to be an eternity. Before we knew it, it was the early hours and we had to make arrangements for the children. I could see that Ian was consumed with emotion so after pulling together a few coherent thoughts, I suggested he go home to sort the children and pick me up some things that I needed. Whatever was going to happen, one thing was for sure, it wasn't going to happen quickly. I was going to be waiting in that room for quite some time. I just hoped it wasn't as long as the wait I had in the back of the ambulance. I was tired and desperately wanted to be left alone with my thoughts if only for a few moments.

As I sat alone, in the midst of a busy waiting room full of people, it was as if time stood still, like I was in an alternative reality. Some tears formed in my eyes, and I took a deep breath in an attempt to contain the emotion that I could feel building like a internal tsunami waiting to consume every bit of life, my life, in its path.

The reality that my life could be over hovered over me like a dense fog. A darkness that was now preventing me from seeing any kind of meaningful future. The only prospect now was death. An end to my time here. It was as if the sand timer that represented my life had now stopped halfway and no matter hard, I shook it, I couldn't get any more sand to fall through. This was it, the end. I had now lived my allocation of days. Life was over.

Having worked as a nurse I had seen many aspects of life and death, but this was different. This wasn't happening to someone else. I wasn't a passenger

on someone else's journey. This was me! I was
being faced with my own mortality. The news was
traumatising, numbing and emotionless. I sat with
a million thoughts swirling around, each one
desperately trying to get my attention. As I sat
frozen, it was only my faith that could penetrate
through the chaos. As the drama of the accident
and emergency room faded, I managed to zone
into a peace and comfort that seemed to somehow
be wrapping itself around me.

As a child I had attended church with my family,
and I still have a strong faith. It was the only thing
in my childhood that had always made sense. It
had brought me comfort and strength in the past. I
believed what the bible tells us about eternal life,
that if we accept the sacrifice Jesus made for us
and make a commitment to follow him then we
will, after our body gives out here, spend eternity
in heaven. Even now I believed and strangely I
didn't fear dying. I knew that my heavenly father
was waiting with his arms wide open and when the
time came, he would welcome me home and wrap
his arms around me and love me with an
unconditional love.

I thought of my family, Ian and the children and I
was overcome with grief, the thought of leaving

them was too much to bear. The tears began to roll down my face, my breathing laboured and again a kind of paralysis overcame me. In that moment I rationalised that they too believed, so although I would miss them deeply I would at some point be reunited with them again in paradise. The thought of the separation was too much to bear so I forced myself to stop thinking about that for fear of being overcome with emotion and pain.

My mind drifted back to the sand timer, and it was then that it hit me.

This could really be it.

My maker, my creator, my father was now literally only one call away. One moment and I could be there with him. Nothing of what I thought had mattered did anymore; financial worries, careers, business, none of it mattered. The gravity that I would soon have no voice, no influence, hit me. I had been given 43 years, what had I done with it? I had a wonderful husband and five great children of who I was hugely proud. But what had I achieved? I didn't feel judged or bad, just challenged. Suddenly the recognition that what I had tried so hard to achieve through attaining degrees, education, business contracts etc, everything I had valued so much, no longer mattered. What mattered was what difference had I made in the lives of others. I had impacted my family and a few around me but what about everyone else? It was too late now. I had been silenced. I was soon to have no voice, no influence, no life. Soon all the people who were sat in the waiting room with me would be getting on with their lives and I would be absent. There would be no re-runs, no second chances, this was it. Life as I knew it was over.

I was eventually admitted to the assessment unit which over the following weeks and months would begin to feel like a second home. It was noisy with beeps and alarms coming from machines in all directions. As I lay on my bed I looked around at the other patients, they were all at least 20-30 years my senior. How was this happening? I thought. It just wasn't fair. I was so young. Okay, I wasn't a saint, but I wasn't out partying every weekend, I'd never done drugs, how on earth had I ended up in this situation?

I was later seen by a different team of doctors who informed me they had looked at the blood results and they were convinced they could sort it. The diagnosis of liver failure didn't mean imminent death, with lifestyle changes I could live with it and even reverse the damage. They reassured me that the liver was extremely resilient and was the only organ in the body that could regenerate itself. I felt as if a huge weight had been lifted and I could breathe. It wasn't all terrible news. I had some hope again and for that I was so grateful.

They arranged for me to have scans to confirm this and advised that they needed to remove the excess fluid that had built up in my body and my abdomen. The procedure would involve inserting a needle through my stomach and allowing the fluid to drain away.

Ian arrived back at the hospital and was so relieved. He had been shaken to the core with the news that I was literally on death's door. We both said that we would live healthier, no more takeouts or snacks in the evening. If nothing else, this was a wakeup call that we had to change our lifestyle. We couldn't continue to work flat out because the result would be., well, it didn't bear thinking about.

Chapter Four

The doctors confirmed through the scans that I had some liver damage, but they were convinced that if I followed their advice all would be well. After a short stay in hospital, I was discharged home with some water tablets called diuretics that would help to reduce the fluid in my legs. A follow up appointment was made to come back to have my stomach drained and I was put on a waiting list to see a consultant liver doctor.

Unfortunately, this admission began a vicious cycle of being admitted, treated and discharged only for my symptoms to persist to the point that I could no longer cope at home, and I had to be readmitted. They had initially diagnosed me with a gall bladder infection with some underlying liver disease. What they missed was that the infection had in fact spread to my spleen and pancreas which would lead to a lengthy course of antibiotics and treatment for sepsis.

My faith in the health system began to tire, they were so under resourced, every admission followed the same pattern where they would pump me full of antibiotics fluids and pain killers and then discharge me home whilst I waited to see the liver doctor. I felt like I was a nuisance, so I tried to make the best of it at home rationalising that if I was really that ill then they would keep me in hospital and stop discharging me and sending me home.

The pain continued to intensify and radiated through my stomach, I felt so tired, so sick. I just wanted to curl up and go to sleep. That, however, was not an option, it was never an option. Having clung on through the pandemic, our business as well as our personal finances were not in good shape. Don't get me wrong we weren't in the same position as many were but having worked every single day with no time off for the last few years we had managed to survive and reinvent our business, but it had come at a cost. Feeling so tired didn't help I could feel myself sinking. Every piece of bad news that came pushing me deeper into a pit of despair and hopelessness.

I was physically and mentally exhausted. With news of the war in Ukraine continuing, energy and food prices rocketing and inflation spiralling out of control. I felt the presence of that darkness that had covered me so many times before. The worry of not having enough; the crushing pressure of not only needing to provide for ourselves but also meet the needs of our five children was almost too much to bear.

I had first suffered with depression when my mum had up and left. My Dad had been flung into a deep depression and struggled to meet his own needs, he certainly didn't have anything left to support me in my grief and sense of loss. I was like a small child who had become detached from her parents. Wandering desperately trying to make any sense of my new unfamiliar surroundings but there was no nice stranger to find me or comfort me before I was reunited with my parents.

There was no going back no restoration, everything

I had now been blown up into a million pieces. I'd been abandoned in the middle of a war zone with no armour, no weaponry, no coping mechanisms no life experience. I had gone to the church we had attended and asked for help. But their answer had been that they didn't want to get involved.

Traumatized with despair and disbelief, I shut them out. All that I had believed to be true now wasn't. I was a walking mental health disaster waiting to happen. With no help and no comfort, the darkness became worryingly comfortable, as if it was tracking my every move sucking in everything I had once found enjoyable, joy and laughter were now a distant memory. There were times when I wished that the darkness that was now permanently present would just take me and end the pain that tortured me.

I again felt the anxiety building, Ian and I had been through more than our fair share of disasters but we always had one common goal and that was to protect our children, to ensure that they felt safe and that no matter what they were rooted in the knowledge that they had two parents who were fighting, I knew that somehow we would get through this.

Before my hospital admissions, I had explained

away my continuous tiredness, putting it down to stress, overwork, and the very real possibility that I was fighting back at the darkness of depression on a daily and sometimes hour by hour basis. That somehow that all too familiar darkness had yet again slipped back in my backdoor and was waiting, waiting for that moment when I turned the lights out in the rest of my house. So that it could move in and set up home in the midst of the storm I was in.

I was determined to stay strong I hadn't come this far, survived a global pandemic for it to grip every fibre of who I was. But it was there lurking in the shadows haunting me waiting for any opportunity to bombard me with thoughts and overwhelm me with fear and anxiety. At times my body would freeze with the fear of the unknown the pressure on my chest became so unbearable I couldn't breathe. So I would, if only for a moment, allow it to take over me and pray that it would pass.

The appointment came for my stomach to be drained for which I was so grateful I was beginning to feel so self-conscious. I felt so nervous as the doctor at the hospital explained the procedure to me. After numbing my stomach, he inserted a long needle into my stomach and as I watch the sheer volume of fluid drain from my stomach into a bag, I was shocked, in total they removed about ten litres. My stomach instantly went from looking Eight months pregnant to near normal.

My new shape lifted my spirits for a while, it at least gave me something positive amid all the darkness that seemed to swirl around me, I finally got an appointment to see a liver specialist. He had all the blood results and the scans. I was reassured that I was doing all the right things, but it would take time to repair my system. He again reiterated that the liver was a fantastic organ and able to regenerate itself. The plan was to review me in three months by which time he expected to see some improvement in my condition.

Reassured, I reasoned that there was nothing more that I could do than to follow their advice and hope for the best. Winter was fast approaching the nights were drawing in and the cold days were upon us, with Christmas around the corner we had a huge amount of work to do. With mounting costs, our business had no choice but to deliver. The stark reality was that I couldn't afford to be unwell. I had to work or risk our very lively hood. And we had worked so hard to get this far. Failure was not an option.

Far from feeling better, despite following a strict regime of drinking plenty of water and a diet high in protein with lots of fresh vegetables and fruit, each day became a struggle. I knew that past traumatic events had triggered a debilitating depression and then, like now, I had been given no choice but to continue. The burden of responsibility weighed down on me like a crushing weight that I couldn't shift. The children were in crucial years at school, and I didn't want to burden them. So I did what I always had done, I stubbornly continued refusing to let this beat me. I would beat it. I would get better.

The news didn't do anything for my state of mind, it seemed that the whole world had gone crazy, inflation was soaring, and our energy and food bills doubled over night; it was completely unsustainable. I had managed it seemed to pick the worse possible moment in history to get ill. The hospitals were at the point of collapse and now we were having to watch every penny, switching the heating off and only using lights when we had to. The fear was almost debilitating, I clung on to my faith. I had prayed in the past and seen my prayers answered. So, I decided despite the circumstances that I would choose to believe and trust however hard that was.

If it was only the physical ailments that I had to deal with then I think I would have been able to cope with the tiredness increasing nausea and pain that radiated my body. It was my mind that was the issue, it was like I was being dragged through a mental and emotional minefield. I was desperately searching for some light in my darkness, my whole world was being shaken and I didn't know what to do to stop it.

The three-monthly review seemed to come so quickly; I was sat in the outpatient department of the hospital patiently waiting for my name to be called. Covid measures were still being implemented so Ian sat outside in the car and waited. I was so hoping that my results would come back better than they had before, I had followed the advice to the extreme. I'd lived like a health fanatic I had never taken better care of myself or eaten as many vegetables! So, I was expecting some good news.

My name was called, and I was directed by a nurse to one of the consultation rooms, the consultant welcomed me and I sat down. After a pause he began, it was not the news that I had been hoping for. Far from getting better my results had worsened. I didn't understand, I questioned the doctor. How could this be, I had followed their advice and taken great care and time to plan meals, to eat well, I'd done my absolute best to remove stress. Ian had taken on a great deal of the pressure from the business, sheltering me from any issues or problems so I could at least try to concentrate on getting better.

The doctor explained that occasionally some people's livers didn't respond to treatment and unfortunately, I was now one of those people. He wasn't giving up hope entirely and he reassured me that there was still a chance that things could recover but we needed to start planning for the worst-case scenario. Apparently, my results were now showing that my liver had deteriorated so much that I was now a potential transplant candidate. He explained that the transplant process was a long one that they needed to start now to give me the best possible chance at survival.

The news hit me like a sledgehammer, how could I break this news to Ian, that my health was so bad that I now needed a transplant in order to survive. We were at breaking point financially and this news would crush him. So, I decided to keep the worst of the news to myself. For now, I would carry the weight and serious of this situation on my shoulders. So, I told him that the news wasn't great, but that the doctor had reassured me and told me to give myself more time. I reasoned that delaying would give us time to get through to the Christmas trading period. Then at least our financial situation would be eased so the news would be easier to digest, anyway there was an outside chance that my body would start to recover though I doubted the doctor's optimism. No doctor would mention referral for transplant if it wasn't the last option.

Chapter 5

I was scared and full of emotion, as I sat watching tv in the early hours of the morning. I was, as was the case for most nights now, unable to sleep. The stillness and darkness of the night only caused me to reflect and analyse every aspect of my life, I could feel life draining from me, slowly, a drop at a time... This was the most serious thing I had ever faced. My family reassured me that they were with me and that I would be ok, but as I sat wrapped in a blanket on the sofa. I felt so alone, no one would be able to travel this road with me. There was no way anyone around be could even start to understand the physical pain and mental anguish that I was going through. How could they?

I researched liver transplantation, it was such a huge operation, even if I somehow made it through the selection process there were no guarantees that they would find a match or that I would be well enough to receive one. I searched YouTube for anything that would take my mind off of my diagnosis and comfort me. I felt helpless completely unable to do anything that would help either me or my family. When faced with challenges in the past, I had always been able to some extent, rely on my own strength and abilities to at least address most of the issues I faced. But that had all been stripped from me this time, there was no letter I could write demanding action no one I could call for help.

It was as if I had been sailing and suddenly a storm hit smashing up the boat I was on, finding myself alone in dark dangerous waters. All I could do was to cling on to any piece of driftwood I could, with the hope that I would float to shore and one day wake on some island on the sand in the warm sun. My faith became that piece of wood, I clung to it as if my life depended on it. Alone in the dark, facing the biggest storm of my life I did, as always when up at night end up listening to Christian worship music, as I lay listening to the words, a peace descended on me and for a moment the waves stopped and the storm calmed just long enough for me to catch my breath and receive the strength to continue clinging on for another day.

I was finding it so difficult to concentrate on anything, a fog had descended on me and everything in my life was becoming more and more difficult. My body was so weak, getting through each day was a struggle; just getting up would exhaust me. I desperately tried to engage with the business and keep the house going but the sickness and exhaustion was overwhelming. By the time I made it downstairs in the morning, all I could do was to sit on the sofa to move any further seemed impossible. I knew that I was seriously ill, I had never felt so ill, and I was frightened.

Even having a faith and a belief system doesn't make you immune from the intensity of emotions felt when faced with the mortality of life. The thoughts of this is it, you're never going to get any better, why don't you just give up now bombarded my mind and soul. I felt so alone. My family weren't stupid and they could see that my health was deteriorating and fast. It was just too hard for even those who had supported me through the hardest of times in the past, to even start that conversation. I had always been strong but despite even my best efforts I was struggling to function on even a basic level.

I was put in a position where I had no choice, take my father in heaven at his word and believe in his promises or give up and lay down to die. For the uncertainty and the crushing pain of a depression that was so eager and wanting to take hold of me was just waiting. If the physical illness and poor prognosis didn't kill me, then this mental anguish that so wanted to consume me, would.

As I again sat and listened to the words of the songs on the tv, I did feel some comfort, I prayed.

God help me. I cried.

This is too much! I sobbed.

I can't do this on my own.

I'm sorry.

I'm at the end of myself and I need you. I whispered.

I asked for help for my family for finances and for the strength to get through this. I had made so many plans, I thought that I'd got everything mapped out, a future taken care of. And then the unexpected had happened my nightmares had become my reality all certainty was gone. My plans left in tatters. I didn't understand why this was happening to me. I was sure of one thing and that was however strong or stubborn I thought I was, I couldn't get through this without some divine intervention. There was no bridge building this time, no masks that I could wear, to hide the truth that I had come to the end of myself.

As I lay on the sofa with tears running down my face, despite the circumstances, deep within me I knew that I wasn't on my own. I had faith, and I would need that faith more than ever now. What I believed was being shaken, I was being stripped to my very core. What had mattered yesterday no longer mattered. I had no guarantees only what God had promised me that he would never leave me or forsake me. He hadn't promised that I wouldn't face hard times, but he had promised that he would be with me. And I had to cling to this hope, it was that or crumble.

We had a big show coming up, if done right the business would net enough money to see us through the early part of the year which was always quiet. I had to try and stay positive but as hard as I tried I couldn't 'just pull myself together' as I had in the past, just to have a shower and get dressed was exhausting. My whole body ached and hurt, my skin was increasingly yellow and bruised with red blood spots and my stomach constantly upset. My gums were continuously bleeding, and my hair was falling out. I couldn't put a brave face on it anymore, the little energy I had was draining away. Lacking any energy or motivation, I would now go days without even getting dressed.

My mental state was awful, the slightest thing was overwhelming. My body was swelling again, I would wake and maybe feel ok for half an hour until the exhaustion hit, every fibre of my body ached, and I had to go back to bed. I was plagued with nose bleeds and would wake to find my pillow saturated with blood as my nose and gums had bled. Most days were now spent feeling overwhelmed with nausea and a pain that continuously radiated across my right side.

I felt increasingly cold, it was as if an icy chill had entered the very core of my body. Whatever I tried I couldn't warm up, I was becoming increasingly unsteady on my feet, and I was forgetting words and getting confused. The slightest thing was crushing me, it was like I was living in a fog, detached at times from reality. I thought that it was because I was so tired but even an exhausted tired me had never forgotten words before. My life was swirling out of control before me being unable to control my mortality was one thing not being able to control my body was another thing entirely.

The business show came and went, it wasn't the success that we had hoped. In any event I lacked the energy to even think about it now. As I sat with Ian one evening when the children had gone to bed, I took the opportunity to tell him about the referral for transplant. I knew that my body was getting worse, and I reasoned that the doctor was just trying to be kind in telling me that there was still hope. I could now barely get through each day. I would get up and if I did manage to make it downstairs, then all I could do was curl up on the sofa.

To my absolute shock he was so pleased, he rationalised that this was a good thing. He had seen me deteriorating and fast. To him this was the answer, the possibility of a new life. All my worries about how he might cope with the gravity of such news disappeared. I explained that I had to go for an assessment and that it wasn't all straight forward. But he didn't care, the news had given him hope and that was enough for him.

Christmas had seemed so far away only a few weeks previously, but it was soon with us, as I woke on Christmas eve, I breathed a sigh of relief. I had made it; I had got to Christmas. Ian would work a few hours in our shop as all shows and online orders had now been completed and then we would finally stop and spend time all together. The last few months had been so tough. Inflation was continuing to rise and despite cutting back on everything our costs continued to rise. We had managed to get the children presents though we explained that there would be no main presents this year, it just didn't seem right to be indulging when so many around us were suffering. The truth was all anyone wanted was for me to be well. We all just wanted to celebrate Christmas free of illness and the pain of not knowing what the future held. Handing out presents however big or expensive wouldn't have made up for the reality that without a transplant, with the rate at which I was deteriorating, I wouldn't be here next year.

For a moment I just lay in bed and rested in the knowledge that the next few days would be spent with those most important to me, Ian and my children. I didn't want anything else, just to have my family close. I loved them all so dearly and it hurt me to the core that I had been so poorly recently and hadn't been able to be there for them as I so desperately wanted to be.

I was determined that day to get up, showered and dressed. I would celebrate Christmas and give the children a great time no matter how bad I felt. As I sat up on the side of the bed the sickness hit me. It was like a disabling weight that strained every muscle causing the little strength I had to drain from me. It took everything I had to lift my body up from the bed and stand to walk the few steps to get into the shower.

The cramps in my legs that had landed me in hospital some months ago, just before I was given the diagnosis, returned. The warm water from the shower eased the pain, but as the water wet my hair and ran over my face. My heartbeat quickened and the tears welled up, I was always trying to remain positive and put a brave face on it, using laughter and humour as a coping mechanism but I couldn't mask it anymore. As I attempted to wash my hair, I wished I hadn't it was so dry and brittle, I watched as clumps dropped down into the water and were washed away.

I desperately needed help, I felt like my body was shutting down. I needed saving, I was at breaking point. Oh God, please help me I cried. What did I do to deserve this, the pain and torment was too much, I cried out God, you have never failed me, and I need you now more than ever, I need you to rescue me. I thought back to the summer and camping, I was now a shadow of my former self.

'God' I cried.

I couldn't even mange the words, I opened my very soul as if presenting him with the mess that I was, this was all I had. This broken failing body and a mind that was even more fragile. I lay myself bear, this is awful I thought, I had never felt so poorly.

'I desperately need your help. Help me please' There were no other options, either he helped me, or I was done.

Little did I know it, but that day would be the catalyst to get the help I so desperately needed. My liver was shutting down, as a result the toxins in my system were building to dangerously high levels; my health was deteriorating so fast, I was so scared. My mouth became warm, and I felt a rush of warmth pulsate throughout my body, still wet from the shower with a towel wrapped around me

I rushed to the toilet, I shook as I was sick. I hadn't eaten anything so there wasn't much to bring up but still my body heaved. Exhausted I managed to control my breathing long enough to catch my breath, as I looked down, I had vomited bright red blood.

I trembled and a numbness descended on me, this detachment from reality had in recent weeks developed into a coping mechanism. As if building yet another bridge over the mess, desperately trying to forget that it was there. I would for a moment feel as if I was being suspended outside of reality, a pause, a moment in time that belonged to just me. The brightness and volume of the blood almost stared back at me and screamed death.

Lacking the strength to even pick myself up off the floor I called to Katelyn who was home. She appeared in the bathroom moments later looking concerned. I just didn't know what to do, I truly felt like I was a the end of myself. A big part of me, just wanted to curl up in bed, pull the covers over my head and disappear in to sleep, anything to escape this hell that was now my reality. Katelyn picked up on my indecision and gently said, 'Mum, you're vomiting blood, we need to get you to the hospital'.

I reluctantly agreed and she drove me to the hospital. It was a familiar route, I felt so tired the only thing keeping me awake was the intensity of the sickness that just wouldn't stop. I so desperately wanted to rest, for this living nightmare to stop, my head throbbed, and a million muddled thoughts raced through my head.

It wasn't long before we arrived at the accident and emergency department, and I began the process of being booked in. I was now a familiar face, and the staff were aware of my diagnosis. I was put in a side room whilst I waited to see the doctor, Ian arrived shortly after, he had shut the business early and rushed to the hospital. He looked worried and wanted to speak to the doctor to get a plan of action as soon as possible.

Christmas I would learn was never a good time to be ill, the already stretched staff were running with a skeleton team. Despite this they were all friendly and the doctor took the time to come and explain everything to us. My liver was now so damaged that the main vein that supplied blood to it was becoming blocked causing the blood to back up and was the reason why I was now vomiting blood. It was called portal hypertension, the pressure in the portal vein was causing the veins in my throat to enlarge and swell, they were referred to by the doctors as varices and there was a risk that they could rupture. The doctor explained that bleeding varices were a leading cause of mortality in people with liver problems and they had to act fast.

I wasn't to have the Christmas that I had hoped for, I was admitted to hospital and scheduled to have surgery first thing on Christmas morning. You know that you are in bad shape when you are first on a theatre list on Christmas day. Due to visiting times, Ian wouldn't be able to visit until later that day. Visiting was limited and it was far more important that he was at home to give the children the best Christmas we could. As I waited for the porters to come and take me down to the operating room for surgery, pictures came through on my phone from home of the children opening their presents and their smiles helped me so much. I had to get through this for them.

The doctor explained the procedure to me, he would under aesthetic pass a camera down my throat to assess the damage, depending on what he saw he would attempt to band any swollen areas to prevent anything rupturing. There were risks, I was being treated at a relatively small hospital and if the procedure didn't go to plan there was a risk that they would have to emergency transfer me to the trauma hospital, which was a short helicopter ride, or a two-hour ambulance trip up the road. I thought of home as I signed the consent form, I had to get through this for them. As they placed an oxygen mask on my face it wasn't long before I was asleep.

The surgery, despite being a success in stopping the bleeding, had required lots of banding and I felt a pounding pain from my throat. I woke in what felt like a daze, I was confused and couldn't quite grasp what had happened. I knew that I was ill and that I was in hospital, but I wasn't sure why. When I tried to communicate with staff, I didn't make sense, I was frightened. I couldn't understand why they couldn't understand or grasp what I was saying.

Unknown to me, I was suffering with a condition known as hepatic encephalopathy. It can occur in people who are suffering with liver failure and is a significant complication of advanced liver disease that is associated with a high risk of death with over 50% of people dying within a year of diagnosis. My liver wasn't working properly, and the level toxins were building up in my blood as my liver was unable to remove them, these toxins were then traveling to my brain and affecting my brain function. The surgery had exacerbated everything, and I was left in a paralysing state of utter confusion.

The doctor asked me a series of questions,

Where was I?

Well, I knew that I was in hospital, it was when he asked me.

Which one?

That the ground opened, and I fell into a crater of confusion and uncertainty.

I didn't know!

Well, I thought I did? but I just couldn't say.

My mind was blank.

Void of anything.

I tried my best to think, but nothing.

The doctor swiftly moved on to the next question.

What day was it?

Well, I didn't know that but I rarely did recently, so I didn't think too much of that! Then the questions continued.

What was the year?

What was my name?

My heart pounded and I was gripped with anxiety. I became more and more agitated.

I didn't know.

Why was he asking me all these questions?

Was he deliberately trying to trick me?

What was his angle?

Why couldn't everyone just leave me alone!

And oh, how I felt so alone, away from my family and isolated from any reality that seemed familiar. I was on my own and frightened. I was confused and disoriented. Still sleepy from the anesthetic I closed my eyes and just hoped for some rest and an escape if only for a moment from this craziness and darkness that was not only trying to take over my body but now my mind. If God wanted me home, then why didn't he just take me and spare me this living hell.

Sometime later my dad and Ian came to visit, they

sat by my bed. I was barely able to communicate but I knew that they were there, and it gave me such comfort. Unbeknown to me, the staff updated them on my condition. They were clear in what they said. I was desperately ill so much so that I was now unlikely to live. Whilst they couldn't accurately predict how long I had, they advised them that it might not be long and that they should be prepared to say goodbye.

As I lay in my hospital bed, frightened to even move, even a trip to the bathroom across the ward caused so much pain and upset. I would come out of the bathroom and be unsure as to where my bed was. I was petrified. A lot of prayers were said for me that night, Ian sat by my bed and put his hand on me and prayed that God would heal me.

Even though I couldn't ask for myself because the toxins were rising so high that any meaningful communication had become near impossible, God heard me and the cries of those most close to me. And he rescued me. As I woke the next day my mind became clearer my blood results improved a little and with medication to help regulated and bring down the levels of toxins in my body and prevent my confusion worsening, I was allowed home.

There was no more the hospital could do, it was clear that my only chance of survival was a transplant. I needed to be transferred to the specialist hospital in the next county who would carry out the assessment for transplant the clock was now ticking, without the assessment there was no chance of a transplant. Unfortunately, it seemed that no hospitals in the whole country had any beds, we were in the middle of winter and the whole health service was overwhelmed.

I had no option but to wait.

Chapter six

My condition didn't change much, if anything it continued to get worse, if that was even possible. I tried my best, but I was so tired all the time I would suddenly with no warning feel the energy drain from my body leaving me feeling exhausted and unstable on my feet. I now rarely left my bed, if I went downstairs, it would take me hours to recover so much so that I began to sleep downstairs. My liver was now so bad that it wasn't storing any glycogen that we all need to maintain our energy, so I had to eat or drink meal supplement drinks every few hours to try and prevent my blood sugars dropping even lower.

I felt so desperately low, I clung to my faith, which was now becoming my everything. I could no longer concentrate on anything, even watching TV had become too much. I became overwhelmed with the slightest thing. Everything was just too much. As I lay on the sofa, after all the children had gone to bed, Ian would set up a bed next to me on the floor of our lounge, so that he was there next to me. Unable to sleep, I watched him as he lay sleeping. I didn't want to leave him; my heart was breaking.

I thought of all the times that I had felt so low in the past that I had wished and prayed that I could just up and leave all the pain behind. But now faced with death, with it just waiting at the door oh so ready to lead me away from everyone I loved so dearly. My heart ached, I wanted to live. More than anything else, I just wanted to live. Death was not the escape that I once thought or dreamt that it might be. It was so final. And what would the cost be to my family and those around me.

It wasn't long before I was back in hospital, my inability to store any energy or goodness in my body was now causing my protein levels to drop which resulted in my body swelling with fluid. It was like I was trapped in a vicious cycle, of transfusions, blood tests and sickness. The doctors were doing their best but if they gave me medication to treat the excess fluid then it would result in my kidney function dropping, and I had now developed diabetes. I was a mess and so desperately needed immediate help.

The waiting continued and I continued to deteriorate. My consultant was becoming more and more concerned that I wouldn't be fit enough to pass the fitness test, that I was required to complete as part of the transplant fitness test. They had to be satisfied that my body was still strong enough to survive a massive surgery. The days passed by, and still there was no bed available at the other hospital. I, as were my family becoming increasingly desperate. Ian asked friends and family to pray, my dad asked his church to pray, which all did. We received message after message from people who were sending their love and support. I can't begin to tell you the comfort that gave to me and my family. To our amazement the next day I received the news that I had been allocated a bed on the liver ward at the assessment hospital and I was to be admitted straight away.

The assessment for transplant would require me to spend a week at the hospital. The information that

I would learn throughout this process, would not only help me to understand what was going on inside of me. But explain why I was experiencing the symptoms I was, which would help enormously.

The liver is in the top right-hand side of the abdomen, of which I was regularly remined of by the pain that would intermittently radiate from that side of my body. I knew that it was large, but I learnt that, it is the largest organ in the body and is the only organ to have a double blood supply and holds about 13 percent of the body's blood supply in any given moment. This I would learn was why I was feeling so cold all the time, when healthy, the liver warms the blood as it passes through. This was no longer happening which was why I would experience periods when I felt tremendously cold and couldn't however hard I tried, warm up.

The liver processes all this blood and breaks down the food and medications it carries into smaller pieces that the body can use more easily, for this reason it is often referred to as the factory or chemical laboratory of the body. It has more than 2000 vital functions mostly to do with storing and breaking down sugars to maintain our energy as well as controlling the building and breaking down of proteins, including ones that help our blood clot and clearing our blood of any poisonous substances including, bacteria and protecting us by producing immune factors.

I was beginning to understand why I was experiencing bleeding and bruising and why I was catching every cold and illness that was around. I was also realising, if I hadn't already, that my liver really was in the final stages of liver failure. The tissue was now so damaged that there was no chance of it regenerating itself. When the liver fails to function people, me included, fall into significant problems.

As the problems were listed in the information I was given, I recognised that I was suffering from all of them. That the fluid overload, bleeding, bruising, confusion, tiredness, and my increasingly yellow colour, that could no longer be explained away as a funny coloured tan, was due to end stage liver disease. I had known prior to the assessment week how serious my situation was, but now armed with the science and knowledge to back that understanding up. I realised that it wasn't just about whether I could get a transplant but how quickly. I was now so sick that I worried I just wouldn't survive the time it could take to get there.

The purpose of the assessment was not just to open the possibility of a transplant, but also to decide whether liver transplantation was the right treatment for me. To assess how severe my liver disease was and to see if there were any treatments other than transplantation that may help. I was to undergo lots of tests that would identify any other medical problems that might complicate or even prevent a transplant being possible. I hoped that they may find an alternative plan. That there might be a treatment that I hadn't heard of yet that would fix me. I was again being bombarded with a million thoughts, outcomes and strategies raced through my mind. I was exhausted, I just so wanted someone to come and take me by the hand and tell me that everything would be ok.

My main concern as was that of the doctors was my fitness for major surgery, they would carry out tests to assess the function of my kidneys, lungs, and heart. I would meet specialist liver doctors, anaesthetists, dietitians, social workers, transplant co coordinators and psychologists. Then at the end of the week or when all the reports from all the professionals were in, they would meet to discuss my suitability for transplant. At which point they may put me forward to the last stage of the assessment which would involve me spending a few days at Kings College Hospital London, to complete the assessment as they would be the ones who would carry out the operation.

This team of professionals held my future in their hands, the decisions made over the coming days would literally determine whether I would be given the chance of life. The thought sent chills through my body, I had to remain positive to get through this. My consultant had been right, there was no chance that I would pass the fitness test in my current state. I was totally overloaded with fluid that had to be off loaded. My feet were so swollen that I couldn't have even hoped to have got my trainers on let alone walk more than a few meters. They informed me that the test would be carried out on an exercise bike, for which I was grateful at least I didn't have to stand!

They prescribed diuretics which would hopefully force the kidneys to shift the fluid, so I would be more mobile, as I was in hospital, they were able to administer this intravenously which I was told was far gentler on my kidneys. They had the desired effect, over the next few days I rapidly decreased in size to a point where I could get on a bike!

As I was wheeled into the exercise room, I was full of emotion. Unlike all the other tests x-rays, bloods, scans monitoring etc. This test had everything to do with me, if I failed this, I not only failed myself but my whole family. If I couldn't pass this, I was condemning myself to death and my children to a future without a mother. The pressure and emotion were almost too much to bear. I felt the tears welling up, and I fought to keep them under control. Masks and monitors were applied, and as I sat on the bike waiting for the technician to begin the test my heart pounded.

I had no choice but to focus 100% on the task ahead.

This was a matter of life!

My life!

I was told that I had to keep the cycle rate above a particular level. As I warmed up and my legs pushed down on the pedals I began to tire as I reached the target. I'd only just begun; I couldn't give up now. This was too important. But I hadn't walked more than a short distance in months, my whole body felt weaker than it ever had, and despite the pain killers I had taken, I hurt everywhere. I focused and I prayed. God, I need you, please help me. With an inner determination I pushed on, I pushed on through the pain, I wouldn't let this beat me. I felt an anger of sorts rise inside of me, this disease would not beat me, this just wasn't fair. How dare it come against me how dare it try and take my life. If I was going down then I would go fighting, I would go with my head held high, with the knowledge that I did my best, that I fought the best fight I could.

I can.

I will.

And I would!

Raced through my mind, fighting emotion and pain I pedaled on. Then just when I thought I couldn't go on for a moment longer, my legs felt like jelly and my body was shaking, my breathing laboured. The technician said the test was over. As my legs stopped pushing the pedals and I came to a stop the emotion hit me like a brick wall. I just cried and cried. I'd done it, the pain was unbearable, but I'd done it. I'd completed the test that the doctors had told me days before I was too unwell to attempt.

I had completed all that I had control over, well in the physical anyway. Now I had to face the toughest part. I had to pass the psychological assessment. They had to be sure that I could cope with the surgery mentally. I had previously disclosed to them that I had been under immense stress during periods of my life, and they would want to explore not only this, but what current emotional and social support I would have. They had to be certain that I would cope with the recovery period and the potential uncertainty of waiting on the transplant list. To assess this, they would want to start at my childhood and have me walk them through my life.

Chapter seven

The thought of trawling through my life petrified me, I really didn't want to explore the inner workings of my mind and lay bare hidden anguishes. I really didn't trust many people, I had been let down on so many occasions that trust was like finding a hidden treasure, rare, if not non-existent. The harsh reality was that either I exposed everything, or I risked not being listed. I had given my body to be assessed and tested, without limitations, that was the easy part. Now it was the hard part.

The truth was that I had suffered with bouts of depression in varying lengths, since experiencing the trauma of my parents' divorce when I was younger. And was currently being treated for uncontrollable anxiety, that whilst the meds they had given me a few years previously helped ease the physical symptoms did nothing for the war that raged in my mind. I had quite possibly got PTSD (post-traumatic stress disorder) that I had never got a diagnosis for as I had an ingrained distrust of any professionals including doctors and psychologists.

I was worried what else they might unearth what diagnosis or labels they would try to pin on me. These people had caused me enough to hurt in the past I wasn't about to put my self in a situation where the hurt of the past could be repeated. Yet here I was, it was a do or die moment. I hadn't been asked about my mental health until now I had just been quizzed about life habits, unfortunately when your diagnosed with a liver condition especially when young it is assumed by many, not all professionals that you're a chronic drug addict, alcoholic with a habit to overdose on paracetamol.

After many questions and tests, they confirmed what I already knew that my liver disease was due to multiple factors and whilst I had enjoyed nights out with friends and had on occasions poured a glass of wine or two too many to relax in the evenings, I wasn't on drugs nor was I an alcoholic! I was just unlucky. But I hadn't looked after myself and my history of mental health was likely to cause alarm bells to ring. It was imperative that I now looked after myself and continued to do so. I couldn't continue like I had in the past, to simply stop eating or eating all the wrong things. Nutrition was key to my prognosis and anything that could affect that needed to be addressed, and if required treated and removed.

They decided not to complete the psychological side of the assessment whilst I was in hospital, they had seen how much the physical test had taken out of me and I was at best emotional. They would let me go home and return the week after. I'm not sure that was the best, well not for my mind anyway. The weeks assessment in hospital whilst stressful at times had allowed my body for the most part to rest. The medications they had given me to ease my confusion were helping and they had also managed to stabilise my fluid retention, I was feeling better than I had in months.

Chapter 8

I was so pleased to be back at home and to finally have some hope, I had passed the fitness test and was now nearing the completion of the first stage of the assessment. I had one more scan and the psychological assessment which were to be carried out on the same day in just over a weeks' time.

The scan didn't bother me, there was nothing I could do about that, it would be what it would be. The phycological side, well that filled me with anxiety and dread. I didn't want to trawl through my past, it had affected me, deeply but I had to. I understood the reasons why, donors were in short supply for every liver that became available for donation there were hundreds of people waiting. I was told that there were over 700 at anyone time and that approximately 69 of those died waiting in the previous year.

There were simply just not enough donor livers for everyone. The emotional demands of waiting for a liver if listed were well documented, living with liver failure was hard enough. The added anxiety of waiting for a liver could make life very difficult indeed. They needed to be sure that I would cope with the mental demands and put measures of support in if needed. I knew rationally that the panic I felt surrounding this assessment was rooted in past hurt, pain and traumatic experiences that if I was honest, I still hadn't healed from. But rational thought doesn't often go hand and hand when the scars of past hurt feel like they are yet again being ripped open. And this scar went to be very core.

So, with a deep breath I started at the beginning, rehearsing in my head what I was going to say. I was determined that however tired and poorly I felt that I would decide what I told them and in what detail. It was true that lots of what had affected me, now didn't, but it had for some time after the events had happened and I now wondered what deep rooted affect that had had on me and my health. What ticking time bombs had been ignited in my past that I was only seeing the effect of now I wondered? This was no longer just about getting listed for transplant, but an exploration of me. I had to get rid of this junk that I was carrying around, it wasn't normal to feel so panicked about what amounted to a chat with someone whose primary goal was to help me and make me better.

I was at college when my parents had split unexpectedly and the fall out had been well, as I would later describe to the psychologist 'messy'.

Messy.

Yes that's the word I would use! and then move on. That would say everything it had to without having to walk back through all the pain and trauma and it was true, that I had to a point, processed the events that had happened some 25 years previously. I had finally reached a place where the feelings of abandonment and loss no longer inflicted the agonising pain that they once did, although it didn't take much to take me back there, to that place which represented such darkness in my life.

I had some years previously, returned to study to

train as a specialist family nurse this involved studying the effects of parenting or a lack of on children's outcomes. I learned that our childhoods have a massive impact on our outcomes in life and that trauma during this period can have a devastating effect on our futures. As I had sat in the lectures listening to case studies and accounts of abuse and the effects that it has. I both realised and reached a new level of understanding about what I had experienced as a teenager.

My mum leaving me so abruptly at such a crucial age when I was only Seventeen and having very little contact with her for years, had deeply scared me. The abandonment and sense of worthlessness cut me to the core. Everything I had known to be true, everything that I had learnt about how families who loved each other and how they were supposed to operate was thrown into turmoil. Despite having previously loved learning and gaining good grades at school, I failed college. The darkness and sadness that penetrated every fibre of my being was almost unbearable.

I had felt like I was being pulled in a downward spiral towards a pit of nothingness. Like something or someone had declared war on my life, the attacks the bombs the strikes were seemingly coming from all directions. Relentlessly, until I was literally left with nothing, living in a battled field where everything had been destroyed, where nothing good existed and love was absent. I learnt that the series of stressful life events I experienced during that period in my life, the loss of a parent, becoming homeless, failing college and the lack of any support triggered a depression that resulted in suicidal thoughts that would stay with me for years.

The year I spent training was like therapy, it was as if it was meant to be. The understanding brought some healing and understanding. Some years after my parents had split, I had found myself in the most awful of circumstances. Having had to navigate life on my own I made some bad decisions which had resulted in my being trapped in an abusive relationship of my own with two young children. I now recognised that I had stayed far longer that I should have done as a result of my own parents divorce. I was terrified that my children would feel abandoned in the way I had, so in some misdirected attempt to protect my children I stayed in a toxic relationship that nearly killed me.

I was so fragile and mentally tortured that by the

time I realised I had no choice but to leave, I was a shell of my former self. The teenager who was full of life, who had ambitions to study and travel the world had long gone, that person was lost, like a ship that had gone off course. I was desperately searching for some direction for some hope that there might be someone, somewhere that might think I was worth saving.

With even the chance of a rescue becoming less and less hopeful in my mind, I was reminded of a time when I had been full of hope. When I had gone to church as a child, I had felt a warmth a presence that I could never of accurately described it was far greater than anything I had known. With out boundaries or limits the love I had felt was overpowering. With nothing to lose I got on my knees and cried out,

'God, if you are there, if you are real then please help me' I sobbed.

My expectations at this point had been a little above zero. If God was still there, which deep down I knew he was, I had to a large extent walked away from the strong belief I had as a child, but I did still believe, but I had been so hurt my view of God and who he was had been distorted and I had believed things that were just simply not true. Little did I know that a little, a fragment of belief was all that was required. Heaven heard my prayers that night and some weeks later I was rescued and able to leave and begin the fight for my freedom.

My leaving provoked a fight that would take me the best part of a decade to win. I didn't know it at the time but my prayers that night enabled me to climb aboard a rescue ship whose course was being navigated by a power far greater than me. Throughout the course of this journey, I would not only get to know the captain, but he became my comfort, my guide, my help and most importantly my friend. His name, Jesus.

As is the case for many women who want to leave an abusive controlling relationship, trying to leave and leaving are the most dangerous. There have been countless accounts of women and children who have been killed in such circumstances. By the grace of God my children and I did not become a statistic but a powerful testimony of how faith and determination can overcome even the most impossibly hostile situations.

As I had sat in lectures, listening to accounts of domestic violence and how to look out for it. I realised how serious my case had been and just how close I had come to losing my life. I still bore

the scars that were the result of being dragged
year after year, through family court proceedings.
As he used the legal system as a weapon to try and
control me when all other avenues failed. I still had
nightmares of being stalked and stuck in my house.
Of having to call the police at all hours of the night
as my ex-partner had turned up drunk shouting
abuse and threating me and my children.

When I had begun a new relationship with my now
husband Ian, the threats and hostility hit a new
level. Our lives had been made a living hell for
years and had only fuelled my depression. There
were often times where I felt overwhelmed and
unable to cope with the pressures of representing
myself in court against a team of barristers. With
my only crime being that of wanting to protect my
children from an abusive drug addict. Who was
eventually jailed, and the court ruled in my favour.

What really struck me was despite the damage that
had been done to me, was how well the children
had done. I had managed to protect them and to
shield them from a lot of the harm. They hadn't
become a statistic; they hadn't failed school. The
opposite was the case they had succeeded
completed university, and both had such promising
futures. I was overcome with the truth that had I of

stayed, if I hadn't of fought year after year then quite likely the opposite would have been the case. And it seemed evident now studying the evidence that they would have led a completely different path, a path much darker and one full of danger.

This new knowledge had helped me enormously, in processing and accepting what had happened and the fight, however painful had been worth it. It had however left me with scars. I still felt feelings of worthlessness and would still battle periods of debilitating depression and anxiety. These traumas were now so deep that even a fresh start and a move to the other side of the country only helped alleviate a little. For the most part I would be ok, but then something would happen. A brown envelope would come through the door, a stay-at-home order issued as a result of a pandemic and like now an innocent assessment would trigger memories, thoughts and an irrational fear in me once again cause me to relive those most awful events.

As I rehearsed past events in my head in preparation for my assessment, I felt challenged. Not in an uncomfortable way, it was as if I were suddenly able to see things from a different viewpoint. I had always viewed the situation through the eyes of hurt and that of a victim. I was realising that by not letting go of this hurt, by rehearsing aspects of it over and over in my mind, the only person that was hurting was me.

The injustice had been huge, but I had not been the only one, hundreds if not thousands of other parents and children had been subjected to abuse. They too had been failed, by the very systems that society had put in place to protect them. The hurt had tunneled so deep in to very soul, that it was only now, staring death in the face, that I knew it was time to hand it over. I would walk into that assessment and tell them my story and once and for all it would be finished.

The day of the assessment came, I was nervous but strangely not anxious. What's the worst that could happen I thought, I was already dying! I spoke about and admitted that the whole court case had made me wary and distrustful of 'the system'. That I hadn't asked for help in the past as quite frankly the help I had received when I had asked had been more hurtful and harmful than help! As I sat in the clinic room at the hospital, the lady conducting the assessment smiled, she seemed nice, but I knew that her view on whatever I said would impact the team's decision as to whether or not I would be referred to the final stage of the transplant decision. This lady, nice as she was, potentially held my life in her hands.

I trawled through what I had spent the last week rehearsing in my mind, to my surprise it just flowed. I knew that God was there helping me, I wouldn't have been, able to do it otherwise, the hurt just ran to deep. I didn't go into massive detail, and that it seemed was ok. She just needed to know who I was and if I was strong enough to endure the transplant process, both mentally and physically. I was in there for just over three hours and as the lady brought the session to a close, I felt relieved but exhausted. Before I left, she asked me if I was offered the chance to be listed on the transplant list would I say yes, apparently some people for a variety of reasons, say no! Without hesitation, I responded.

'Absolutely, yes' I explained that I would view it as a second chance at life.

One that I would embrace and live to the full. No longer would I wallow in victimhood but embrace all the opportunities that life has to offer, that I wouldn't look back but seize the gift I was being given and live! I had reached up and taken that box off the shelf for the last time, no longer would it haunt me, no longer would it have any power over me, enough was enough. This time the box and all its contents would be thrown into a fire and burnt until nothing was left. As the door clicked shut behind me, I left the hurt and pain that I had carried for so long with her in that room. I hadn't got the energy or will to carry the pain anymore. However long I had to live, transplant or not, I would live the rest of my life free and finally at peace.

A few days later, I received the call that I had been so apprehensive about. The team had met and discussed my condition looked at my scans and considered my fitness test and psychological assessment. And they had decided to refer me to the final stage of the assessment. I would be going to kings in London. They would have the final say and make the decision to list me, this news meant, I was 90% there. I felt a huge weight lift, this was it! I was on my way. My hope and determination that somehow this would be ok was restored. I would with their help fight this thing.

Chapter 9

The wait to get to kings would not be with put its issues, despite my newfound freedom and optimism, I was becoming increasingly sick, and the doctors were finding it increasingly difficult to keep me stable. My electrolyte levels were everywhere and my protein levels despite their best efforts kept falling, which were yet again causing my body to swell, the colour of my skin to become even more yellow and the sickness was almost unbearable. I continued to be back and forth to the hospital for treatment.

It wasn't long before I received the call inviting me to kings, I was to arrive on the Sunday and stay until the Wednesday. We had it all planned, Ian would drive me the 300 miles from our home up to London. Where he would come with me to the ward before leaving me for a few days whilst I went through the last steps of the assessment. He would stay with is parents and try, if possible, use the opportunity of a break from the children to get on top of the mounting paperwork for the business.

Kings was huge and very impressive, far grander than either one of my local hospitals. The building where I would be based had been opened by Queen Elizabeth II some years earlier. The liver ward where I would be based for the next few days was located on the first floor, on a long corridor that was dedicated to all things liver related. They even had their own dedicated liver operating rooms and ITU. I learnt that it was the best and the largest liver transplantation unit in Europe. If they couldn't sort me then no one could.

Once they had settled me in and shown me to the room where I would be staying, the assessment began almost immediately, they lost no time in taking bloods, some were repeat tests of ones I had already done previously and some extra ones. They also asked if I would be part of a clinical trial looking at the link between sepsis and liver failure, to which I agreed. I had suffered with a heart murmur since I was born so they conducted some extra tests on my heart, to ensure that it would be strong enough for surgery. The process was stressful, the staff were lovely and welcoming, but I knew how important this was and felt the anxiety building.

As stressful as it was my stay at Kings soon ended, my heart pounded as doctor after doctor entered my tiny hospital room. All eyes were on the consultant, the moment I had been waiting months for. The consultants reassuring smile put me at ease a little, well enough to pause, breathe and listen to the verdict.

Then in an instant he spoke the words I had so longed to hear.

"We are going to list you for transplant" he said.

He explained that the decision would be finalised that Friday, when the whole team met, but it was all but decided. I was going to be given the chance to, if a donor was found, live. It was as if he was handing me a get out of jail free card, gifting me with another shot at life. There was a long hard journey ahead of me but there was now a glimmer of hope, the door to my future had been opened.

The consultant went on to explain that the current approximate time on the waiting list was three to twelve months, but that it could possibly be sooner. As this news sunk in, one question came to the forefront of my mind, it was a question that I had pondered a lot for the last few weeks and that despite my best efforts of searching the internet, I had not yet found an answer too. So after a pause and a deep breath I took the opportunity to ask the consultant and the team of medics that surrounded me.

I asked what my life expectancy was if I didn't get a transplant. He clarified that I wanted a figure, to which I nodded and told him with absolute certainty that I wanted to know exactly how serious my condition was as whilst a year waiting didn't seem like the end of the world, I was very well aware that my physical symptoms were getting worse on a near daily basis, and I was concerned that I wouldn't be well enough to survive a massive surgery in a months' time let alone a years' time.

He responded that I had an approximate 50% chance of surviving a year.

I thanked him and he left.

The clock was ticking, but there was now hope. I just had to concentrate on doing my absolute best to stay well enough for surgery, so that I would be ready whenever that lifesaving phone call would come inviting me to come and receive my gift of a new life.

As Ian picked me up and we began the long drive home, the news gave us a new hope and the chance of a new beginning. The whole process had taken its toll on both of us, he was desperately trying to keep the business going and look after the children and house, whilst I was so poorly and supporting my now frequent hospital stays. Whilst we were both so overjoyed that I was going to be listed there was no denying the fact that the only reason I was being listed in the first place was that the medics believed that my long-term chances of survival depended on it. There were other patients on the ward at Kings who had been told that they did not yet meet the criteria needed to be listed, or who were offered alternative treatment. Transplant really was seen as the last option.

There was one last hurdle to complete, I would attend an online educational session the following week where they would walk me and others through the process of transplantation and the process of being on the list. Once completed my name would be placed on the national liver transplantation waiting list, at which point a transplant benefit score would be calculated. This scoring system would be used to match available livers to patient's most in need that would have the most benefit.

I would learn that, whenever a donor liver became available, the national Blood and Transplant service would carry out a matching run, considering both donor and recipient characteristics. That liver would then be offered to the patient who had the highest Transplant Benefit Score on the national waiting list. The transplant surgeons would then assess the liver offer for the patient to decide its suitability. If for any reason the offer was declined, then the liver would be offered to the next patient on the list.

The morning of the session arrived, I felt so poorly, and I was so worried that I just wouldn't have the strength to sit through the session as it was likely to last over a few hours. Ian set the computer up for me, in our downstairs bedroom where I now spent most of my time. This meant I could just sit up in bed and Ian made sure that I had drinks and snacks to hand. I was constantly having to make myself snack or my energy would plummet so low that I could barely function, let a lone sit through hours of education. I desperately wanted to engage, I wanted to know but even holding a short conversation with my family would now exhaust me.

The session was conducted as a group, as I looked at the image of me staring back, from the computer screen, I turned my camera away so the others couldn't see. All the other participants, despite being listed for transplant all looked so well in comparison, I on the other hand didn't look well at all, I looked swollen and yellow. I looked like a dying liver patient. I just needed to get through this and then I would be listed and the wait to receive the gift that would save my life would begin.

Chapter 10

I was exhausted but still wide awake, it was the early hours of the morning, and I was still up. Unable to sleep, I desperately tried anything to distract myself from the nausea and pain. I had really had, had enough, it seemed that there was no end to this torture that had become my existence. As I looked up I saw my packed suitcase by the door, it was there ready to grab and go if got the call to say that they had a liver for me. I checked my phone again, there were no missed calls. I don't know what I had been expecting I'd only been on the list a few days and I had been warned that it could take months, and even then, I had to be prepared for false alarms. The liver might not turn out to be an exact match it might be damaged and not fit for transplant, the list of what ifs continued and on. I'd heard many stories of people getting the call travelling all the way to London only be told that the liver wasn't viable, was too big or wasn't a complete match after all. It was heartbreaking but part of the journey I as were they, now on.

I knew that my body was in rapid decline, I'd felt awful for months, but this was different, it felt as if my body was shutting down. I was full of emotion and numb at the same time, as if suspended in a sea of nothingness, I didn't know how I should feel, what I should process. All I could do was concentrate on not being sick. To think was too much, I was well beyond any kind of rational thought now, my brain wasn't thinking clearly enough. My mind had shut down to cope with the basics and right now that was just getting through each hour, each day and night in any way I could.

Suddenly that all too familiar feeling washed over me, and I was sick, to my horror I had again vomited bright red blood. And it didn't stop. Ian heard me in the bathroom and came to see that I was ok. When he saw the blood, he too panicked, and got straight on the phone to the hospital. Mine was a familiar name to them at this point, so they immediately realised the seriousness of this new development, they advised Ian to call 999 for an ambulance. Unfortunately, this course of action would result in me being taken to our local hospital, which wasn't ideal, and we didn't want to risk another lengthy stay in the back of an ambulance, I needed to be seen by the team of liver doctors who knew me who had assessed me and who had a direct line to Kings in London.

Ian had no choice; he informed the hospital that we would be beginning the near two-hour drive to the other hospital and prayed that they would have a bed for me when I arrived. The drive was long and stressful, roads had been shut to allow for overnight roadworks and diversions were in place. The sickness continued and I clung to the bowl on my lap as Ian drove us as quickly as he could. As we drove, I coughed and spluttered, still the blood continued to come up. Ian kept offering to stop, I could hear the panic in his voice, but I refused. I knew that this was serious, and I wanted to get to the hospital as quickly as we could, the sooner an expert saw me the better.

As we arrived at the hospital, they welcomed me and reassured us that they would do everything they could. The usual rounds of tests commenced, but I was relieved that we were being seen by familiar faces and most importantly by doctors who were experts in their field and were all well aware of my prognosis. I was sent for an endoscopy which involved putting a camera down my throat to assess what was going on. It confirmed the bleeding, it was happening due to ulceration of the original surgery site and thankfully they managed to stem it. That at least was some good news.

After we had waited a while the consultant came to see us, this time it wasn't good news. The blood tests had shown that my kidneys were struggling, and my sodium levels had again fallen, which was why he explained, I was feeling increasingly sick, the levels had dropped well below the level they needed to be for surgery. Bottom line, if I was called now for transplant, then I wasn't fit for surgery.

The room went quiet, the consultant paused as if to give us a moment to process the news, It was Easter weekend which meant that there was a bank holiday on the Monday. He explained that normal protocol in these situations was for him to inform kings and they would then pause my place on the list until I became well enough to be placed back on the list. As the words exited his mouth, I tried my best to ignore them with the hope that they might just somehow disappear.

I felt an all too familiar lump form in my throat, yet again my life was being held in a spiral of uncertainty, my one chance of life seemed to be escaping and there was nothing I could do about it. Sensing my emotion, the consultant tried to reassure me that they would do everything they could. He explained that there was time to sort it, because of the holiday break they had a few days to try and as he put it 'patch me back together' before they would have to let Kings know on the Tuesday.

We still had a window of opportunity, I had no option but to have hope, without that I truly had nothing left. I was so poorly that that I was moved to a bed opposite the nurse's station. A place reserved for only the sickest of patients so I could be observed. Everything was becoming increasingly hard, the fluid in my body was rapidly building again and the pressure was making it increasingly difficult to breathe. I could no longer lay down and needed to sit up in bed or the crushing weight and pressure of the fluid would make it impossible to even take a breath.

To even take a few steps would cause my whole body to ache with pain, lifting my swollen legs became agonising and exhausting. Despite my best-efforts eating was becoming unbearable. If I did manage to push through the insufferable sickness, then I would only be able to eat the tiniest amounts as the pressure from the mounting fluid in my abdomen on my stomach was now colossal. I had been given some meal replacement drinks which at best tasted awful, but I was encouraged by the staff to view them as medicine, which I did my best to do, trying to take regular sips to get some nourishment. I understood if I didn't eat anything then I could very quickly go downhill and my life saving surgery would become less and less of an option.

I could no longer get off the ward as I had in previous stays. I had found the hospital stays so hard, the noise and being separated from my family was, well like a living hell. I had never liked being on my own, but being separated from those you love when you're at your most vulnerable was one of the if not the worst experience of my life. It was if I was on a ship at sea who had lost its course, floating aimlessly clinging to the hope that one day, maybe one day help would come. Praying that the next storm that hit wouldn't be the last. As I lay upright in the bed, my headphones became such a comfort to me, I could put them on close my eyes and disappear. Escaping for a moment from the noise of the machines and from watching the other patients around me.

As Tuesday came, so did another set of results. The consultants came to see me on their morning ward round. It wasn't good news. My blood results were showing that despite a very slight improvement my kidneys weren't good, and my levels were still below what they needed to be for surgery. They had had no choice but to inform Kings in their meeting early that morning, Kings, whilst sympathetic had advised that they would wait another 24 hours for my results to improve but if they didn't then my place on the transplant list would have to paused until I became well enough to be relisted.

I was so weak that it was almost too much to even cry, a numbness engulfed me and despite the doctor's kind reassuring words a knowing that this might be it descended on me. I knew that my life was ending. I was swollen and yellow, I looked like a person who was being poisoned from within. As I put my headphones back on, I escaped back to a place that had become so comforting to me. The time for regrets, what ifs and maybes were over, all I had left was my faith.

The peace and love that I felt during those hours was immeasurable. I didn't know if I would live or die but I knew beyond all doubt that there was a God far bigger than me, who did have a plan. Whether that plan was for me to be well or to enter heaven I didn't know but I knew that either way he had me. I had no fight, no strength left all I could do was put my life in his hands.

Ian was staying nearby and visited every day; he would come, and we would laugh as he brought me another blanket. He had tried so many times to bring in so much food, anything that I might be able to even take a small mouthful of, but as my appetite dwindled, he brought me lovely blankets instead. I was always so cold, and they helped me to keep warm. As he sat and held my hand, I could see that he was on the edge. He would encourage me and tell me of all the friends and family members that were praying for me and make me smile with the news of what the children had been up to. As he left that day tears welled in my eyes, I wondered how many more days we might have or if I would ever see my children again.

Another day came and went, and my blood results

had improved a little, but a little more that disastrous was still a terrible result. I felt powerless, there was nothing more I could do I had put my trust in God, and I left my situation up to him. Ian had text to say that he was just waiting for some clothes to dry in the dryer where he was staying and then he would be in. Knowing how poorly I was the ward were letting him in to see me outside of visiting hours for which we were both so grateful.

Whilst I lay listening to my music, the consultant appeared at the end of my bed, I hadn't realised that it was time for the ward round already. As I pulled the headphones off my head so I could hear, she told me that she had just got off the phone to kings, my bloods whilst still not great had improved enough for them to consider surgery. Then she paused and told me the news that I had been so wanting and praying to hear.

They had a match.

They had a liver!

For me!!

I was overcome, I suddenly had a surge of strength and got up threw my arms around her and thanked her.

"Oh my goodness, thank you, thank you Jesus" I cried out in pure joy. I knew that this could only be the hand of God, for my results to improve at the exact same time a liver became available. This was a miracle and an answer to so many prayers.

The doctor explained that they were organising an ambulance to blue light me up to London which was over a four-hour journey from where we were. And that I should pack everything up ready to go. I was ecstatic, I called Ian straight away, he burst into tears on the phone he was overcome and overjoyed. He said that he would plan for the children and meet me in London.

It was all go, there was literally no time to waste. The nurses helped me pack my things into my bag, and as I waited for the ambulance crew, I couldn't quite believe what was happening, the enormity of the surgery before me didn't even enter my mind, I was being given a chance at life and that was all that mattered.

Chapter 12

The ambulance crew arrived, within about fifteen minutes! There was a man and a lady paramedic. As they approached my bed and checked my details, I thanked them for coming to get me.

'It's our pleasure' The lady smiled.

'We live for calls like this, we haven't had one for a few years!' she exclaimed.

She was so happy that they were able to help, the enormity of what was happening began to hit me, as they took me down to the ambulance, she chatted away probably to calm my nerves. She explained that they were both ex-military, now working for the ambulance department. And they were both so excited to be helping me. What I was going through wasn't everyday run of the mill stuff, this was huge. As the ambulance pulled away from the hospital and the blue lights and sirens were activated, I again thanked God for his help. This could have only been an answer to prayer, a miracle. I had only been on the transplant list for 6 days! For my results to have improved just enough to be surgery ready at the exact time a donor liver became available well there was no other explanation, the prayers of many had been heard and answered.

As I looked out of the window I saw the fields, the grass, and the sky, passing by, I was so thankful. It had been so long since I had been outside or aware of my surroundings, I was continually vomiting blood the last time I had travelled anywhere. The crew continuously made sure that I was comfortable and monitored my condition. They were able to give me regular updates so that I was able to let Ian know our progress. It was a lovely dry day and the traffic flowed so there were no hold ups.

After driving for a few hours, we entered the outskirts of London, the traffic became more congested and despite the blue lights it was slow moving. Knowing how time critical my arrival at the hospital was the crew were becoming frustrated at the other road users, who didn't seem to care that an ambulance was trying to get through the now gridlocked roads. To all of our delight we were joined my two police cars who cleared the traffic and escorted us through the traffic until we were almost at the hospital. It was unbelievable as if I was a bystander in a movie, as we travelled through London alongside the river Thames it was if an army had been deployed from heaven, one that I couldn't see but that was guiding my steps and was clearing the roads, escorting me all the way through.

As we pulled into the hospital there were buildings and people everywhere, it was lucky I was in an ambulance, because there was no where to park! The crew took no time in getting directions to where I needed to be and wheeled me up to the ward, where I had been a few weeks previously for my assessment. I had a friendly welcome and was shown to a room where my observations were taken, and a doctor came to take bloods. They were carrying out all the initial checks and they would be back to check on me in a while.

I watched as a doctor came to take more blood; my arms were both nearly entirely black from bruising. My blood just wasn't clotting and the number of tests that they had carried out over the last weeks and months had meant that it was now nearly impossible to locate a vein that would produce the amount of blood they needed for all the pre surgery tests they needed.

Thankfully he managed to get the blood he needed, and I watched as vial after vial was filled via a needle in my arm. It wasn't long before Ian arrived, he had driven up and left his car at his parents who lived about a one-hour commute away from Kings so he would be able to stay there for as long as he needed. Although nervous, he was overjoyed at the prospect that I could be receiving a new liver and he sat with me as we both anxiously waited for more news and details of the next steps.

It was now early evening and the staff informed me that they were doing final checks and tests on the donor liver to ensure that it was all healthy and wasn't carrying any potential diseases. I was told to shower and wash my hair with some antibacterial scrub and prepare for surgery. I did as they asked, scrubbing my body to ensure any germs were gone.

As I lay on the bed, all gowned up and ready for surgery, trying to rest as best I could, we began to worry. Why was it taking so long? We had been warned that there was every chance that it could be a false alarm, that the liver might not be entirely healthy or not a complete match.

We did all we could to keep our minds off of the what ifs, but I knew deep down that this was my chance. My health was deteriorating so fast that I wouldn't survive another wait. My clock was ticking, I was finally just about well enough to survive surgery. It truly was now or never. Later on that evening the doctors returned, they explained that they had done all the testing that they could and that it was now or never. I would be heading down to surgery within half an hour.

The transplant coordinator who was a specialist nurse overseeing my care, explained that I would be going down to theatre at any moment. My heart raced; this was it. It was really happening. We walked the short distance across the corridor to the operating room. As I peered through the window, I saw all the surgeons, nurses and other health care professionals all getting ready for my arrival. There were a team of doctors who would be responsible for removing my diseased liver, another team would then take over and attach the donated liver. There were also two anaesthetists, specialist nurses and other technicians, the room was full of people, all there for me.

Within a few minutes of arriving one of the surgeons and an anaesthetist came out to ensure that I understood why I was there and what was about to happen. Once they were satisfied, they said that they would give Ian and I five minutes, before they took me through the doors and into surgery. The thought of waiting even one more minute filled me with dread,

'It's OK' I said.

'I just want to get on with it' I turned to Ian hugged him, told him I loved him and followed the doctor into the operating room, where I climbed up on to the operating trolley, lay down and they placed a mask over my face, and I went to sleep.

I had been warned that there might be complications, it was a huge surgery, and it didn't come without its risks. That was one of the reasons that they had to undertake such a comprehensive assessment process. Even though I knew the risks, it did not once occur to me that there might be any serious complications. I understood I would suffer pain and it would be a slow recovery process, but I had put my faith in God and in the skill of the surgeons and trusted them completely. But as I lay unconscious there was an unseen battle going on for my life.

The transplant coordinator explained to Ian that the surgery could take hours and that he would be better off going home and getting some sleep. It was now the early hours of the morning, and it wasn't safe to be outside in central London, only the week before a nurse had been stabbed outside of the hospital. So, he called his parents, and they picked him up. After some hours he received a call from Kings to say that the operation had been successful and that I was being moved to Intensive care as per the plan to be monitored and kept stable for the next 24-48 hours. Relieved he was able to get some sleep before he woke early to catch the train back to the hospital.

Still sedated on the intensive care unit, one of the nurses who was looking after me noticed that one of the drains was filling with blood. She immediately called the doctors. Fresh blood was literally draining from my body. Having already lost a large amount of blood during surgery, about four liters in total. They worked relentlessly to save my life, I urgently needed to go back into surgery, so that they could identify the source of the bleed and try to stop it. My life hung in the balance; I was losing blood at such a rate that they couldn't replace it fast enough. They needed to stabilise things, as to rush me back in to surgery without first replacing fluids, blood and platelets would risk me bleeding out, and my lights going out forever.

Some hours later with the surgeons ready they managed to stabilise me enough, by pumping me full of fluids and platelets, to get me back in to theatre. The staff called Ian, to let him know the news. He was at the train station waiting to board the train to come and see me. Although they remained calm Kings explained to him that I was being rushed back into theatre for another surgery. He was told to make his way to the hospital and go straight up to ITU. In a state of shock, he called my parents and rushed as fast as he could to the hospital.

When he arrived, I was still in surgery, and he had to wait not knowing if I would live or die. He said that it was if his whole life fell apart in an instant. He had been so strong, but this was too much. With no one with him for any comfort, he prayed. Unconscious and in theatre, I wasn't aware, but many people were praying, it was as if an army of prayer warriors had received the call. The war was not one in the natural but in the unseen world. There was a battle raging, a darkness that was trying everything to advance and take me. To silence me to end my life, to ensure that I wouldn't live another day.

Across the country, my family my parents, aunts, uncles, cousins and a family of faith many of whom I had never met, all got to their knees and got others to join them. They stood on the promises of God and cried out to him for his intervention for the darkness to be disarmed and for my life to be spared.

After another five hours in surgery, a team of medics pushed me back across the corridor on a bed to ITU, nurses either side were still working on me, I was in a medically induced coma. Too poorly to be woken up, they wheeled me past where Ian was sitting and on to the unit. He hardly recognised me, I had tubes and machines everywhere, my body had swollen beyond recognition, and I was badly bruised.

'That's my wife' he cried.

The surgeon intervened and took him to one side,

he explained that during the first surgery my diaphragm had been torn and that there was also additional bleeding from behind my liver, my whole abdomen had filled with blood. He was confident that he had managed to identify and stop all the bleeding but as a precaution they were preparing the team in case I had to be rushed back in. He explained that I had come within two hours of dying that I had lost over 8 litres of blood and my kidneys had stopped working. My condition was critical.

As Ian sat with me, he watched three nurses working nonstop to try and stabilise me, he said that it was as if I was still in surgery. I had tubes and lines everywhere; a machine was breathing for me and there were lines in my neck and arms. I had also been put on dialysis to filter and clean my blood as my kidneys had stopped working, without this I would die. Ian was told that he could hold my hand. So, he sat helplessly unable to do anything other than hold my hand, he said that it was the worse day of his life.

Many people say that when in a coma they can still hear what is going on around them. It's hard to put into words exactly what I experienced in those days that I spent in a coma. I was present but unable to communicate, a spectator of sorts to my own condition. I could still hear. I couldn't explain it other than to say it wasn't a dream, I was very much awake. Aware of another realm, another state of being, there were people talking all around me. As if suspended in a type of sleep but aware of noises and aware that there were people around me.

There were people everywhere.

I knew that I was paralysed, I couldn't move and there was nothing I could do to move closer to the voices. I just tried hard to listen to try and zone in, despite the noise, to what they were saying. I had no understanding into why I couldn't move, neither did that bother me. All I wanted to do was to hear and make sense of what the voices were saying.

As I listened, there were different people, different groups talking to one another. As one group finished a conversation another would start. The subject matter always the same, some spoke of God others of Jesus, Christ, others of church. I remember thinking that it was the nurses and that they all must go to church. That kings must somehow attract countless Christians into employment. But I was aware of people everywhere. Its impossible to explain what I truly experienced into words; they simply don't exist. I knew, with every fibre of being that I was ok, I wasn't scared, frightened, or concerned. A constant peace washed over me. Deep within me, even my paralysed state, I knew that I was safe.

I later realised that the voices I heard were angels who were present in response to prayer. The prayer was affecting change in a realm I had heard of before, but never experienced like this. As I lay in a coma it was as if I was suspended in a place that was neither here nor heaven. It was a battle ground where the weapons were prayers and the soldiers, prayer warriors whose words had such power that they changed the course of my life forever. I was heading for death but because of their prayers, God heard them and released his angels to fight on my behalf, which saved my life. Their belief held me when I was so weak, when every body function was being controlled for me. They spoke for me and cried out to a God of miracles for help and healing.

Suddenly I was gagging, and gasping for breath, disoriented and dazed. I tried to make sense of my surroundings, I thought I was in recovery, and was relieved that the surgery was over. Breathing was a struggle, it felt like I was drowning, a mask was being held over my mouth which felt awful. The air was pressurized, each breath was a huge effort and exhausting. Like a drill sergeant a nurse kept telling me to breathe, the noise and alarms everywhere were overpowering. I was sleepy and just wanted to close my eyes and be left alone but every time my mind drifted the monitors would sound as my oxygen levels dropped. The nurse would get me to breath and count as I struggled to take each breath it was strenuous and draining.

With every breath I became more aware that I was on my own, I felt vulnerable and managed to catch my breath enough to ask for Ian. The nurse explained that it was the early hours of the morning and that he would be back later. I didn't believe her, knowing Ian would have never of left me I became convinced that she was lying to me. My anxiety escalated, I didn't trust her, and repeatedly asked for Ian. I knew that I could trust him, and he would know what was going on.

I was drifting in and out of consciousness, I would sleep for a few minutes wake and be convinced that a day had passed, and Ian still hadn't come. I couldn't understand why he wasn't there. Hardly able to breath for myself and unable to even attempt to move my body I was at the mercy of everyone around me. I had no energy nor was I able to shout for help. I was scared, frightened, and felt so vulnerable. After what felt like a lifetime he finally came and hugged me so tightly, I just cried and cried as he wiped the tears from his eyes.

'You've been in a coma' I looked at him confused.

I tried to speak but as I tried to grab the oxygen mask and remove it from my face the monitors again alarmed, and the nurse told me to breathe. I could feel the force of the air flowing into the back of my throat, it was a horrible sensation. Each breathe such an effort. As I became more anxious, desperately trying to understand what he was saying to me the more the alarms rang.

'You have been unconscious for days, they had to take you back into surgery for a second time' He continued.

I didn't really understand what he was trying to tell me, I was still on such high levels of drugs that I was still floating in and out of a sedated state. I tried to talk, again trying to take the mask off but the monitors would alarm, and they were so loud. So, feeling safe with Ian there I closed my eyes and fell back to sleep. I continued to drift in and out of consciousness for a few days. With my condition stabilising I was able to start having some fluids. The relief I felt as Ian lifted a little sponge soaked with water to my lips. My lips, mouth and throat were so dry, it was as if I had been sleeping in a desert for weeks pounded by the sun and dry heat. In an instant the cold water quenched a thirst like I had never felt.

Chapter13

Just as London is described as a city that never sleeps, the same was the case in the intensive care unit, it too never slept. And as the sedation wore off neither did I.

My condition was still critical and involved constant monitoring. I was becoming more and more aware of my surroundings. Realising that they were fighting a losing battle with me and the mask they gave me oxygen via my nose which much to their relief, I was able to tolerate.

Breathing on my own meant that I had to keep practicing deep breathing and cough to bring up anything that might settle back on my lungs and cause unwanted problems such as pneumonia. The physiotherapists came to assess me, they were kind and reassured me that they would be helping me with my breathing and to get me going again as soon as I was able. As part of their assessment, they asked me to lift my arm. I didn't even give it a second thought, of course I could do that! but as I tried my whole arm felt like a dead weight. It was as if it belonged to someone else, I had no control over it at all, I was hardly able to lift my arm more than a few centimeters. Sensing my concern, they again asked me to lift my hand whilst they positioned their hand on top, I was to push as hard as I could against it. Again, there was nothing, I was unable to do it. All power had gone. It was frightening. I was so very fragile and felt so vulnerable.

Assuring me that it was perfectly normal they left, with tears in my eyes I tried to cough. The pain was excruciating. The nurse gave me a pillow to place over my stomach which, she said, if I held on to whilst I coughed would help. I tried but the pain was so intense it overwhelmed me and left me speechless. My chest rattled for what seemed like hours before I was able to cough up the small amount of phlegm that was causing me such distress.

As one lot of staff handed over to the next the days blurred into one, with no windows and the lights always on, the only way I knew whether it was day or night was by the chart hanging up by my bed, which stated the day of the week if it was morning, afternoon or nighttime and the name of the nurse looking after me. Without this I would have had no idea of what day or time it was, the time dragged on and on. Nights were the worse, although I had a nurse with me nearly all the time I felt so alone.

My lack of strength meant I couldn't even use my phone. Ian had left it for me and despite it only being on the table Infront of me, as I tried to take hold of it my hands failed to grasp it. My hands behaved as if they were made of jelly. If I managed to get hold of it I would drop it again with in seconds. I was so frustrated, but it was the lack of control that made me feel so defenceless. My dreams were so frightening and vivid that I became scared that I was going crazy.

When I did manage to get to sleep, I would dream that I was travelling at speed towards a cliff edge, I would reach the edge and fall towards the sea. My throat hurt and it was as if I was being suffocated and unable to breathe. One afternoon, I woke from sleep screaming. Petrified that I was falling to my death I was crying out for help. Some staff rushed to me thinking that something was very wrong, I was sobbing and sobbing overcome with emotion. After comforting me they explained that it was all the emotion and that I was remembering and reliving the surgery. Whatever it was, it was too much, I was broken physically and mentally. My body throbbed with pain and now I felt mentally tortured and undone, too frightened to go back to sleep I just lay quietly and cried.

With my kidneys still not responding to treatment I was to stay on dialysis and remain in intensive care. I was now able to sit next to my bed in a chair, which I was encouraged to do daily to decrease the risk of chest infections plus it made me feel better. Despite trying my best to remain optimistic, I was struggling with managing the pain and being stuck inside. I had always liked being outdoors and would always suffer in the winter when the weather and the short days meant that we often stayed inside in the warm.

One morning the nurse who was taking care of me that day, asked if I would like to go outside. It was a nice sunny day and she thought that it would make me feel better. I hadn't even realised that it was an option! So my response was absolutely! We waited

for Ian to come at visiting time, and they helped
me into a chair. I must have looked a sight as all the
drains, monitors and syringe drivers for pain relief
were loaded onto the back of the chair. I was under
strict instructions to let the nurse know straight
away if I felt ill in anyway.

It was only a short distance along the corridor to
the lift, as I was wheeled out and I looked up and
down the corridor I realised that it was the first
time I had been there since I had walked into the
operating room opposite, how much had happened
in a few days. As we approached the doors to the
hospital, I could feel the cool breeze as the doors
opened and shut, it was paradise compared to the
dry sterile air in intensive care. The nurse parked
the chair, and I was able to sit and look at my
surroundings. It was central London but despite
their being buildings everywhere the hospital had
tried their best to make the surroundings pretty, in
between the car parks and drop off points that
were situated in between the buildings there were
bright flowers and plants. I couldn't tell you what
they were, I've never been much of a gardener, but
they were pretty and made me smile.

As I looked up at the sky it was blue with fluffy
clouds moving slowly across the sky. I turned my

head and there it was, the sun, I could feel its heat on my face, and it looked so radiant and alive. Tears again welled up; Ian looked concerned.

'I so nearly wasn't here' I said as I squeezed his hand with mine.

'But I'm alive' I managed to say, before the weight of emotion silenced me from saying anymore.

We both looked at the sky and were quiet for a moment. As I again cast my eyes over my surroundings I again looked up and on the top of a tall flagpole I saw a flag flying. It was the Union Jack. In that moment I realised how blessed I was to be British. There was much wrong with my country but regardless of what darkness and bad news the media were portraying, when I needed help my country and its health service they stepped in, and they saved my life. If I had been born in another country, then I quite likely wouldn't have had access to any health care and if I did then I wouldn't of been able to afford the monumental amount that my surgeries must have cost. And I thanked God for my country and for the first time I truly felt grateful and proud to be British.

I felt a wave of exhaustion pulsate through me, seeing the colour drain from my face, Ian and the nurse took me back to the unit, the trip out finished me, but it lifted me so much mentally and was exactly what I needed. Being on the unit, although isolated in a cubical of my own, I was aware of the other patients. There was a man next to me who had also had a transplant. He couldn't have been much older than me maybe five to ten years at the most and he had children. He too had additional surgery following the transplant surgery, but his outlook didn't seem too good. I would see his wife walking past the end of my bed as she went to visit him, in the next bay to me, as the days pasted, she was looking more and more upset.

I would smile and, on a few occasions, if I felt well enough ask her if she was ok, she said that she was holding on, but the tears I heard from up the corridor as she sat with her husband told a different story. As the tears turned to deep heart wrenching sobs one afternoon, I knew that it was bad news and I felt a grief descend on me, I felt to deeply for her and their children for they had just lost their dad, but I also felt torn in two for my own. That had so nearly been me, her torturous cries had so nearly been Ian's. After I had reflected on this for some days, I decided that I was going to make the most of this gift of life that I had been given. From now on I was going to live life to the full, do all the things I had planned to do and never got around to doing. One day at a time I would get stronger, I would walk again, get home to my family, and live the best version of life 2.0 I could.

With a newfound motivation I was in full on fight mode. I had wasted far too much of life down and depressed and in a constant state of worry to what the world might throw at me. It was time to fight back to take my life back and embrace the future once more. Yes, I was in so much pain but as was the case in child labour I would, as I once got told by a fantastic midwife, push against the pain, and use it to progress forwards. From now on it was onwards and upwards!

By this point I was told by the doctors, that I was now able to eat, and although I had no appetite at all, I ate. A few mouthfuls to start with and then before long I was able to eat a small plateful. The doctors and nurses were so pleased with my progress and their support and encouragement helped me so much. Apart from a couple of trips to the front doors of the hospital, my life now revolved around my bed and chair. With lines in my arms and neck and drains coming out from either side of my abdomen. I couldn't take more than a few steps away from the machines for fear of pulling the lines that my life depended on out of my body. With my body still swollen beyond recognition and my legs about 4-5 times the size they should be moving anywhere was painfully agonising and limiting.

If anyone pushed down on my swollen fluid filled feet, then they would leave an imprint. Shoes were out of the question. The only thing that would fit on them was the hospital issue nonslip socks which had XXXL printed on them. The staff reassured me that the fluid would come off it would just take time. Every day the doctors conducted a ward round of all the patients on the unit, there were so many of them you could hear them coming, crowded around the bed, and led by the consultant a team of doctors, nurses, physios and other professionals would discuss my progress.

I was eager to get off all of the machines and monitors that I was connected to. they were so limiting, and I was determined to try and walk, I saw this as my ticket off the unit and beginning my journey home. The plan was once I was well enough to be discharged to the main liver ward I would stay there for a few days before I would be discharged back to the hospital, that had previously looked after me so I could be closer to home.

Then one morning as the doctors again crowded around the end of my bed, I got the news that I had been so longing to hear, they were going to trial me coming off the dialysis machines, to see how my kidneys got on. If all was ok, then the plan was to get be back to the ward within a few days. I was so pleased. The staff on the unit were all so nice, but the constant noise was getting to me. I just couldn't sleep. I hadn't slept more than an hour or two in weeks and before that I was convinced that the only reason, I slept was due to the medication. I felt anxious and on edge the whole time, even when I did get to sleep, I woke worried that I was again suffocating and unable to move.

True to their word within a few days I was back on the ward, where I had begun the whole journey to surgery some ten days before. So much had happened, it now felt like a lifetime ago. It was strange being in my own room without a nurse constantly present. Whilst I was so pleased that the intense noise had finally stopped, it was the first time that I had been alone for weeks. Before I had got to Kings I had been under constant observation at the other hospital. But now it was just me and four walls. It all felt so unreal, like it had almost happened to someone else. Less than two weeks before I had been worried that my days were numbered but now although still in pain with and with a long road to recovery ahead of me, I was alive, it was almost too much to process.

The one thing I had been longing for was a shower. I hadn't had one since the night before the surgery and I had dreamt of day when I would be able to wash my body properly. Never again would I take the little things in life for granted, being able to make a cup of tea in the middle of the night when I woke unable to sleep. Or to walk to my own toilet or shower. A knocking on the door interrupted my thoughts, a nurse had come to take my dressings off for the first time. They had checked my wound before but today was the day that the dressings would come off for good.

As the dressings were removed and I looked down at my scar. It saw that it started just below my ribcage and followed the line down to just above my belly button. Where it split in two one line going left and the other right, so it covered the whole of my lower abdomen spanning from one hip to the other. It was a large scar, I wondered what I might tell the children. I recalled how my own Dad had explained a scar he bore on his left side due to kidney surgery when he was a young adult when I was a child.

He would tell the story of how he suffered terribly whilst swimming in a river in Africa, when he encountered a crocodile that he managed to wrestle and whilst he survived, he was left with an almighty scar from the bite he endured! Of course, I knew the truth, but the story was fun and I loved hearing it. As I ran my finger from the top of my scar to the bottom and then to either side, I figured that the crocodile story wouldn't really work for me! In any event there weren't crocodiles roaming the streets of London so that wouldn't have worked at all! My children would have seen straight through that, I laughed at the thought.

Then paused.

It was the first time I had laughed in a very long time, the thought of seeing the children and being able to make them laugh again filled me with such joy.

I decided that the story to the children would be that whilst in London I got mistaken for a traitor to the crown and had been accused of treason, so I was hung drawn and quartered like in medieval times but miraculously I was spared my life! I smiled, I knew that would make them laugh or at least roll their eyes! I couldn't wait to see them all again, I had missed them all so deeply it hurt to even think of them. I hadn't wanted them to see me so poorly, it wouldn't have been fair on them, and I was too frail and sick to have coped with it.

Ian had sent them pictures and relayed messages from me, so they were all kept informed, but my current reality had been too difficult to share. I was their mum and supposed to be strong and brave and for so long now I hadn't been either. When I saw then I wanted to be able to hug them and tell them that everything was going to be ok. That life 2.0 had begun and that the future looked good and was full of adventures and surprises.

As Ian visited that afternoon and helped me lug my swollen body to the shower, I thanked God that I had got this far. As I looked in the mirror for the first time in weeks, I wasn't shocked. I looked tired, swollen and poorly still, but my eyes. My eyes had turned from yellow to white. They hadn't looked like that for months. I looked to either side, but however much I inspected them, the whites of my eyes were just that, white. It didn't matter that my lips were cracked or that my hair was so brittle and dry it looked as if it was all about to snap off. The picture of my eyes staring back gave me such hope. Life had returned. Behind the skin and the muscles, my new liver was working, it was doing its job in filtering all the toxins out of my body and slowly, a day at a time, was repairing the damage that had been done. As I sat in the shower with the water falling on my head like a waterfall, I cried.

I was alive.

Chapter 14

I only spent two nights back on the ward before I was on my way back to the Southwest. The nurse in charge came to tell me early one morning that they had arranged an ambulance car to take me back to the hospital. I was overjoyed, I called Ian immediately and told him not to come up that day but to make his way home instead. He too was so happy and couldn't wait to let the rest of the family and the children know the good news.

As I was wheeled out of the hospital with my bags by the nurses and helped to get into the back of the car, I was relieved that I was able to find the strength to get in and that my swollen body fitted. I was still in a lot of pain from the surgery and was suffering from terrible back and leg pains but as the car pulled off and I begun my journey out of central London, on to the motorway and towards home I sighed a deep sigh of relief. As the buildings became more sparce and were replaced by open spaces and fields as far as the eye could see, I could almost smell home. As one nurse told me, I was now over the worse and I held on to that.

As I arrived back at the hospital that had been like a second home to me for the last few months, I realised how far I had come in only a few weeks. The last time I was there I was fighting for my life, waking everyday with the desperate hope that today would be the day that a liver would come available. I wasn't out of the woods yet there was still a long way to go but I was nearly home. I hoped that I would only be a few days and that they would let me home.

Unfortunately, I was to learn that what I wanted, and the reality of my situation were too completely different things. The novelty of being back amongst familiar surroundings soon wore off and I was faced with day after day of being stuck in the same room, looking at the same four walls. To make it worse I had a clock opposite me on the wall that only seemed to make time go even slower. Despite it being easier for my family to get to see me now, my mind was more alert and active than it had been in months I was getting bored and frustrated.

As the toxins began to clear, my ability to think and reason returned. It was as I had been viewing life through a fog and that fog was slowly clearing until it finally lifted. Every so often the door would open and another staff member who had helped me over the previous months, when I had been so poorly, would pop their head in to see how I was and express how happy they were, that I was alive and well. They couldn't believe how well I was looking, and it made me realise quite how ill I had been, when the call had come some weeks previously.

My pain medication had been downgraded, but I was still in agonising pain in my back and legs. The doctors were putting it down the sheer amount of fluid I had carried and was still carrying. They prescribed some diuretics which would help to shift the fluid more quickly. They wanted to see me up and walking and stable on my new anti-rejection medication before they would let me home.

Although all my liver results were looking good, they weren't going to leave anything to chance. I would have to take anti-rejection drugs for the rest of life. To stop my own body's immune system seeing my newly transplanted liver, as foreign and activating the rejection process to destroy it. Daily bloods were taken to check the levels of these drugs in my body, they had to stay within a particular range if they were to drop to low then I would run the risk of my body rejecting the liver and that was something everyone wanted to avoid at all costs.

Even though I was on a huge dose as the blood results came in the levels kept dropping, they reassured me that this was all perfectly normal and expected at such an early stage. The side effects were horrible, the tremors in my hands made it difficult to take hold of anything and the headaches and sickness were awful. I knew that the side effects should settle or at least lessen so I tried hard to stay positive.

The nights were long and hard, the pain in my back and legs would build as nighttime came and the darkness drew in, I tried everything to stop the pain. I put films on listened to music anything to take my mind off the intense pain that radiated my lower body. As the hours ticked past, I would watch the clock longing for the time that I could again ask the nurse for some more pain relief. The problem was that what they were giving me really wasn't working. It was strong and would literally knock me out for a few hours but when I came to the pain would be there like a raging fire ready to engulf and consume me with pain again.

I would wake and cry with the knowing, that when I tried to move the pain would flood my body. I explained this to the doctors, and they eventually changed my pain medication to one that worked. I was convinced that it was a nerve type pain, I had been warned that I may never get the feeling back in my lower stomach as the incision severed all the nerves but only time would tell. With the new pain relief, I was able to get up and walk a little which helped in shifting some of the fluid and as the weight came off, I was able to move more easily and freely.

I was desperate to see the children I hadn't seen them now for so long and even before that I had been so poorly that I was barely present even when I had been home in between hospital stays. The doctors suggested that whilst I needed to still be in hospital that if my next blood results were ok then I might be able to go home for the weekend. I was so excited, and it lifted my mood tremendously. I would be able to see my children and my dog. Who I had missed so much.

He had layed with me on so many occasions when I was up late at night, it was as if he knew, he sensed that something was wrong. He would jump up and lay next to me on the sofa, placing his chin on me and staring at me with his big eyes, it was as if he could see deep inside me and knew everything. I didn't need to say anything but just be. He was there keeping me warm and providing me with company.

As I received the news that the bloods were ok and I could go home, I called Ian. He picked me up a few hours later and we began the drive home. The last time I had been a passenger on that journey I had been clutching a bowl and being sick. Now although I hurt and couldn't walk far, I was a million miles away from that traumatic journey whose memory still sent shivers down my spine, how close I had come to death. It was almost too much to contemplate.

It was a two-hour journey back home, so I watched how much I drank before we left. Even if there had been somewhere to stop on the way back there was no way I would have made the even short walk from the car park to the roadside services. Plus, I had to be incredibly careful about infection. If I was to catch something now it would be awful. The high levels of immunosuppressants I was on made me so vulnerable to catching anything. The children and Ian had spent the last few days cleaning the house so it was as clean and as germ free as it could be.

As I arrived home and looked up at my house, tears welled in my eyes, there had been many times when I questioned if I would ever make it back here at all. Ian opened the door and I slowly walked into the front room and sat down; everyone was so pleased to see me. My Dad who had been looking after the children greeted me with a big hug and then one by one the children all hugged me and I despite having tears in my eyes I reassured them all that whilst my recovery would be ongoing and it was a long road back to full health, the surgery had gone well, and all was going to be ok. I told them how proud I was of all of them, especially my youngest as she was only thirteen and I knew that it had taken its toll on her. As I sat hugging her, I was so grateful, this really was life 2.0 and I was going to embrace it with all I could.

Fortunately, we had a downstairs bedroom as

there was no way I was going make it too upstairs. As I lay under a duvet in a comfy bed, I was so thankful to be home, I slept for more than a few hours for the first time in weeks. When I woke, I was able to get myself to the kitchen and make a cup of tea. Something I had only dreamed of doing a few weeks before. I remember thinking to myself that I must never forget these times, that even as the normality of life returned, I must not forget to be thankful for the small things, as I now appreciated how quickly all of these things that we take for granted, can be taken away.

I did nothing other than sit, watch films and spend time with my family that weekend it was wonderful. As the time came to go back to the hospital, however grateful I was for the wonderful care that they were giving me, I couldn't help but feel like I was being taken back to a prison of types. The whole building represented so much pain for me, I had spent so many nights suffering in pain and in mental anguish, worried that that day might be the last, that I just wanted to stay at home. Ian was great and reassured me that I would be fine that it would only be for a little while longer and then I would be home for good, and we had such an amazing future to look forward to. As we began our drive back to the hospital, I prayed that he was right.

It wasn't until we were back at the hospital that I realised how tired I was, the weekend although fantastic in so many ways had been exhausting. Even the car journey had been hard, I'd felt every bump and crack in the road despite Ian driving as carefully as he could. As I got back into my hospital bed that night I thought of my children and Ian, I really was so blessed to have such an amazing family. We had all been through so much, but we all remained united and together. Together we had faced the battle and together we would rebuild our lives. One stronger and full of character.

Thankfully I was only back at the hospital for a few days before I was discharged home, I could of stayed longer but the team had seen how much better and happier I was after a few days home so they allowed me to go. I was to return weekly to the clinic for the foreseeable future to have my bloods and general health checked. My medications would still need to be tweaked weekly until everything had stabilised and to ensure that if anything untoward was happening then it could be dealt with and sorted early before it became a problem.

As I packed my bag with all my clothes which

mainly consisted of pyjamas and jogging bottoms and my toiletries, I looked out of the window at all the cars coming and going. I was about to make my journey home for the last time, yes, I would have to come for appointments, but my stays here had come to an end. I wasn't going home this time with the anticipation that I would be returning within a few weeks, because I had yet again deteriorated and become too poorly to manage at home.

This time I was going home with a road to recovery in front of me a path of opportunities, yes setbacks may come but they would be nothing like the nightmare we had all been through. It was now about making the most of everyday, stepping forward pushing boundaries. Embracing potential, dealing with challenges, and seizing the opportunity in every day.

Chapter 15

I had to share my story.

A living breathing testimony.

What I had been through wasn't just a story.

I still believe that all things are possible with God, my healing and recovery could not of been accomplished by my efforts or even the amazing skills of the doctors alone. What I experienced was divine intervention there were far too many hurdles and coincidences that couldn't be explained away. Every part of my journey although painful fell into place perfectly. Some would say that the universe aligned perfectly. No longer would I use bridges and masks to cope with the difficulties in life, the storms would come but instead of coming up with a solution I would instead keep my feet firmly on the ground and call out for help.

I knew beyond all doubt that it was down to my relationship with Jesus, I was far from perfect and had made many choices that I regretted but underneath all the mess and drama I loved Jesus, he had rescued me so many times. And it was because I loved him because I acknowledged him, that he reached down and not only rescued me, but he held my hand and carried me through some of the worse days I have ever experienced.

He had set before me an open door; the open door was transplant surgery. Little did I know at the time that not only would I be receiving a new liver but a new understanding, divine insight and an experience that would change my life forever. An experience that wasn't just for me but for many others who are searching for the truth. I hadn't learnt a theory, I'd experienced the miracle working power of God, I'd walked it, seen it, felt it and heard it, when I had no strength left and I was at the end of myself both physically and mentally he opened the door, and I walked through.

For more information, please visit www.notinthebox.co.uk

Printed in Great Britain
by Amazon

29128511R00088